Creativity and Feature Writing

Creativity and Feature Writing explores how to generate ideas in feature writing. Using clear explanations, examples and exercises, experienced feature writer and teacher Ellie Levenson details how feature writers and journalists can generate ideas and how to turn these into published, paid-for articles.

A variety of approaches to idea generation are explored, including getting feature ideas from:

- objects, your own life and the lives of others;
- the news and non-news articles, including the internet, books, leaflets and any other printed matter;
- press releases, direct contact with charities and press officers;
- new people, new places and new experiences.

The book draws on a range of tips from practising journalists and editors and displays case studies of example features to chart ideas from conception to publication.

Ellie Levenson is a freelance journalist and lecturer in journalism at Goldsmiths College, University of London. As a freelance journalist, her work has appeared in many publications including the *Guardian*, *Independent*, *The Times*, *Financial Times*, *Daily Express*, *Cosmopolitan*, *Easy Living*, *Times Educational Supplement*, *Local Government Chronicle* and *New Statesman*. She also runs journalism courses for www.journalism.co.uk and for think tanks, businesses and other organisations.

She is the author of two non-fiction books, *The Noughtie Girl's Guide to Feminism* (2009) and *Fifty Campaigns to Shout About* (2011), as well as two books for children.

Creativity and Feature Writing

How to get hundreds of new ideas every day

Ellie Levenson

Routledge
Taylor & Francis Group

LONDON AND NEW YORK

First published 2015
by Routledge
2 Park Square, Milton Park, Abingdon, Oxon OX14 4RN

Simultaneously published in the USA and Canada
by Routledge
711 Third Avenue, New York, NY 10017

Routledge is an imprint of the Taylor & Francis Group, an informa business

British Library Cataloguing in Publication Data
A catalogue record for this book is available from the British Library

Library of Congress Cataloging in Publication Data
Levenson, Ellie.
Creativity and feature writing: how to get hundreds of new ideas every day /
Ellie Levenson.
pages cm
1. Feature writing—Handbooks, manuals, etc. 2. Journalism—Authorship—
Handbooks, manuals, etc. I. Title.
PN4784.F37L48 2015
070.4'4—dc23
2014047672

ISBN: 978-1-138-79963-9 (hbk)
ISBN: 978-1-138-79966-0 (pbk)
ISBN: 978-1-315-75596-0 (ebk)

Typeset in Sabon
by Book Now Ltd, London
Printed in Great Britain by Ashford Colour Press Ltd.

MIX
Paper from
responsible sources
FSC® C011748

With thanks to Richard, who is a supportive husband.

Contents

Acknowledgements   ix
How to use this book   xi

Introduction   1

PART I
How to get ideas   5

1 What is an idea?   7

2 Getting ideas from objects   21

3 The Lego example   27

4 Getting ideas from your own life and the lives
   of your friends and family   36

5 Getting ideas from the news   54

6 Getting ideas from other (non-news) articles,
   including books, leaflets, the internet and any
   other printed matter   71

7 The magazine example   85

8 Getting ideas from people you don't know, places
   you've not been and things you haven't done
   before   99

9 Getting ideas from press releases, and from direct
   contact with charities and press officers   113

PART II
You've got an idea, now what? 125

10 Finding a hook 127
11 Key components of your article 139
12 Pitching and writing your article 153

Appendix: Ideas! 159
Glossary 165
Index 167

Acknowledgements

Many people have helped with the writing of this book. Many of my journalism lecturer colleagues at Goldsmiths, and other institutions, have given invaluable advice and support, and I am also hugely thankful to everyone who has given their stories and tips for use throughout this book. Thanks, too, to everyone who has given me a feature idea, whether deliberately or unwittingly, and to the entire team at Routledge.

How to use this book

Whatever stage you have reached in your journalistic career, be it a seasoned editor or an as-yet unpublished freelancer, or anywhere in between, this book should refresh the ideas side of your brain. It looks at several ways to get ideas for features, suggesting methods of thinking about subjects and asking questions, so that your brain starts to generate hundreds of new ideas every day, and then guides you to think about whether these ideas are viable as features (many won't be – and that is okay) and how to work out who your audience will be and then pitch your idea. Also covered is a look at the types of feature there are and the popular components of features, for those with feature-writing block or wishing to jog their memories regarding the different ways of writing features.

What this book doesn't do is teach you to write. It assumes that you can put a sentence together and understand how to use basic grammar, and that you have some sense of what kind of writing works journalistically.

But, if you are a feature writer wanting to expand your ideas repertoire, an editor wanting to refresh the ideas you are commissioning, a blogger wanting to generate regular content or any other kind of writer or editor in need of ideas, then this book can help.

Each chapter in Part I looks at different ways of finding ideas, and the book can be read in a linear fashion, reading each chapter and completing each task, as a masterclass in finding ideas. Or you can dip in and out of pages randomly and still find inspiration for your own ideas. Part II then looks at what to do once you have your idea, from finding a hook to researching experts, pitching your idea to editors and writing the article. Finally, the Appendix offers 100 prompts to kickstart your idea generation process.

Introduction

What a privilege! In what other career can you contact a world expert in a subject, introduce yourself for the first time and have a reasonable expectation that they will tell you everything you need to know about their subject in language that you can understand?

Being a feature writer is a brilliant job. At its best, you develop an interest in something and it itches away at your brain until you decide to scratch that itch by finding out everything you wanted to know about that subject. You then get to digest the information, challenge it, think about it and write it down for other people to then be impressed by your expertise. And you can do this about absolutely anything you are interested in. Wow.

Even at its worst, short deadlines, low pay rates and commissions to write about things you don't really care about, a good feature writer should find points of interest. In fact, it is your job to find points of interest.

If you are the kind of person who can dismiss an entire subject as boring, with no interesting aspects whatsoever, feature writing may not be for you.

But, if you can find interest in everything, even things that don't necessarily excite you in your own life, then read on. For example, golf may not be your favourite subject. As a sport you may find it incredibly dull. Maybe you can't name a single professional golfer currently on the circuit. But, if you could conceivably find interesting how many miles someone walks playing the average round of golf, or why so many business deals take place on the golf course, or who designs the shape of the bunkers, or the probability of getting a hole in one, or links between golf and diplomacy, or where the factory that manufactures the majority of the world's golf balls is, then you have it in you to be a feature writer.

And if you already find golf fascinating but you can't think of anything duller than shopping for women's shoes, you should still be able to find interesting the condition of the workers who make the shoes or the animals who become the leather and glue, or how the shoes that people wear can influence how they are perceived in the workplace, or the links between footwear development and sporting records, or the physical disabilities caused by ill-fitting shoes and the cost to the nation of treating these.

Not that there are any guarantees. The average freelance journalist probably won't get to talk to the President of the United States on the phone. But if they put in the call to see if they can talk to him, they might be passed on to someone else powerful or fascinating (or even both). Or they might end up writing a piece about the bureaucracy of the White House press operation. Either way, something will come of it.

Throughout this book I have tried to show how the thought process works for coming up with ideas that can be turned into features. I am writing about all kinds of features for all types of publication, from traditional print media such as monthly consumer magazines and daily newspapers, to websites updated hourly, personal blogs and sites that operate like a traditional magazine, albeit online. Whether you are a freelance feature writer, a blogger or an editor keen to refresh the ideas you have for the pages you look after, this book should help you.

Not every thought will become a feature, however. In my freelance writing, I work on the assumption that only one in every ten or so ideas that flash into my head will be worth taking further and working into a pitch. And of the ideas that become a pitch and get sent to editors, perhaps one in five will get a commission (not necessarily from the first place it is sent, of course) and become a feature article. That means that to get one commission I need to have 50 ideas. However, if you have hundreds of feature ideas every day, as you should after reading this book, then those numbers stack up pretty quickly. So, I haven't edited the ideas that have occurred to me while writing this book, as I want you to be able to see how ideas occur and develop, including those that do not make the cut. Therefore you shouldn't be too surprised if reading this you raise an eyebrow and think to yourself, 'Well, that will never work'. When that happens, which will be frequently, try instead thinking, 'How could I change that idea to make it work?'

Ideas are everywhere. Every time you see something and think 'that's interesting' or notice a new trend or wonder why something happens (Why do Rice Krispies go snap, crackle, pop? Why don't all countries drive on the same side of the road? Why are accents so different?) it is a potential feature idea. Once you get into the 'idea zone' it's as if you hear voices in your head all the time saying 'That's interesting', or 'I wonder why that is'. You have to actively switch that off for a break, rather than turn it on for ideas, and even then some pop through if they are too interesting to ignore. Basically, you need the confidence to know that if you think it's interesting then it's interesting.

As an example of how absolutely everything should be giving you ideas, once you get into the right mindset, try reading this short introduction again and seeing whether it sparks any ideas for features in your mind.

Here are three to start you off...

- A feature about how people react when they do meet the President of the United States or other world leaders.
- How to become a world expert (on any subject, however small).
- How did the size of golf balls and balls used in other sports become standardised?

Task: Ideas from the Introduction

Start as you mean to go on and see if you can come up with five of your own:

1 _____
2 _____
3 _____
4 _____
5 _____

Part I
How to get ideas

1   What is an idea?

Before you can come up with feature ideas, you first need to know what a feature actually is.

Unfortunately, it is a very hard concept to define – I haven't managed to find a satisfactory explanation of a feature anywhere else that is worth replicating here.

First, let's think of what a feature isn't. A feature is not a news story, a comment or opinion piece, a review or an interview, though it may contain some elements of all of these. That is, its primary purpose is not to tell you something new is happening right now (news does that), nor to tell you what an individual thinks about a specific subject (comment does that), nor to give an opinion about a piece of work (a review does that), nor to give you a picture of what someone else thinks in response to specific questions (an interview does that).

However, many features will contain elements of all of these. A feature may include a new trend or be in response to something that is happening at the moment, give you the writer's opinion on an issue, pass comment on a piece of work or interview people about a subject and include their responses.

So what marks a feature out as a feature, rather than as one of those other categories? Well, the aspects of other genres included in features only appear as elements of a bigger piece of work. A feature will combine some of all of these genres to make a wider ranging article.

As a general rule of thumb, a feature will also do two things:

1   It will make you an expert in a specific (often narrow) subject.
2   It usually answers a question (though this is often implicit rather than explicit).

If you are not sure whether your idea is a feature, try applying these two rules. Ask yourself what subject the reader will be an expert in after reading it, and what question (or questions) your feature is trying to answer.

The BBC news website (www.bbc.co.uk/news/magazine) has a Magazine section full of features. Its style is often to use a question as a headline or subhead, which also doubles as a link through to the article.

On the day I am writing this, seven articles are flagged up on the front page of the Magazine section. Four of them have questions as a header or subhead:

- *Brazil noodles? – Just how genuine are Brazilian themed products?* (to tie in with the 2014 Football World Cup).
- *Generation Right – Are young people more right-wing than their parents were?* (in response to a report that claims this is the case).
- *Face value – why does scarring continue?* (about facial scarring traditions in West Africa).
- *Line of consent – should you ask someone's permission to kiss them?* (in response to a trial of an MP, in which he said claims against him were the result of a clumsy pass rather than sexual abuse; he was acquitted).

Although it is rarely the job of the journalist writing the piece to come up with the headline, it can be helpful to write yourself a headline in this questioning style to keep in your mind as you write your feature, so that you can focus on ensuring your piece sticks to its narrow subject and answers a specific question.

Although this question need never make it into the final copy, or onto your editor's desk, it should come through clearly enough in your article that a reader, asked to identify what question your feature is answering, would come up with the same question you had in mind when writing it.

Task: Find the subject and question

Go through any publication that prints features. See if you can identify the narrow subject and the question being answered for each one.

Narrow subject	Question being answered
Scarring traditions in west Africa	Why does this tradition continue?

Task: Make the headline a question

Look at all of the features in a publication. Rewrite their headlines and subheads so that they ask a question.

Original headline	Rewritten headline

One of the reasons it is so hard to give a pithy one-liner defining what a feature actually is, is because there are so many different types of feature.

When you are sending a pitch, it is often best not to be too prescriptive about what type of feature you would like your idea to become, because if you suggest one specific type to an editor and they have another type in mind, it might just be easier to reject it outright than to commission you.

However, it is a good idea to be familiar with some common types of feature, so that you can think about how you would approach any articles you pitch, in case an editor asks you this, and so that you can target publications that publish features in styles that you enjoy writing.

The names I have given each feature type here are just ones used by me, so please don't assume that editors or other journalists will know what you mean by them should you also use these names. As your portfolio of features grows, you may choose to categorise features differently, or come up with styles that are unique to you.

Also, it is worth noting that lots of feature definitions you may read elsewhere talk about how features always tell a story. Features do indeed often tell a story. But not all features do. In terms of definitions, I'd say features that tell a story ... well, they are the ones that tell a story. Features that don't, don't.

List features

This kind of feature is a list of different ways to do something, though the number, format and thing can differ – for example, 50 ways to find a man, 37 ways to boil an egg, what your pen says about you, viruses you should be scared of, London's coolest new restaurants, common illnesses to watch out for in your new kitten, etc. In the past, lists would always be a multiple of five or, preferably, a multiple of ten. At the moment, however, the trend seems to be for lists of random length – perhaps so that journalists can prove they are only including what they really believe should be listed, and not adding things in for the purposes of achieving a round number.

Personal essay

A feature based on your own experience that goes on to explore the subject in more detail – for example, a personal exploration of falling in love, moving to the South Pole, changing career, putting on a play, having children, etc. This doesn't necessarily have to be 'deep' – it could be your experience of aid work in a war zone but it could also be about your experience of trying a new kind of fitness regime.

And personal essays are not always in essay form, as such. I recently saw an article where the writer explored their relationship through looking at the receipts they had kept during their life and talking about what they spent and where and when and the significance of this. This kind of feature allows you to be particularly creative in form and content.

Experiential/reportage

This differs from the personal essay because it is written with the journalist as an observer rather than an active participant. This kind of experiential feature, also known as reportage, uses words to paint a vivid picture so that the reader can get as close as possible to feeling as if they too are experiencing what is being written about – for example, a night in the life of the accident and emergency department of a hospital, what it's like to sleep rough, walking the Santiago de Compostela, watching open heart surgery, etc.

You can either do this kind of article openly, as a journalist, or undercover, without telling people you are a journalist. A very good example of this is a piece by Carole Cadwalladr from the *Guardian* headlined 'My week as an Amazon insider' in which she got a job at a warehouse belonging to the internet shopping company Amazon, and wrote about what she found there.

News feature

An in-depth examination of a news story looking into the background of what is happening and giving analysis and expert opinion. This differs from news, which just reports new developments and actual events, as it delves deeper into the story and adds colour (that is, the small details that make what is being described seem more real).

Case study based feature

Using a specific story, usually of a person but it could be of a business or an event or something else, as the basis for a feature – for example, a feature on divorce that uses someone's personal story as the thread running through the feature. Sometimes the case study is separate and runs alongside a feature exploring a particular angle of the subject, such as an article looking at how to protect your finances in case of divorce with a true story of a specific divorce alongside as the case study. A subset of this type of feature is the 'Freak show' – a 'look what happened to me (or the person I am writing about)' feature, sometimes written as a first person piece, sometimes not – for example, how I lost ten stone, here's a person with no limbs, this child survived falling into a cage of lions.

Multi case study based feature

As above, but with more than one personal story.

How to...

This can be anything from how to make a fruit cake, to how to change your life by retraining or how to achieve world peace. This kind of article can combine real life experiences with step-by-step processes. I would actually say that many features fall into this category, more than you first think – business sections often include 'How to start a business' articles, finance sections look at 'How to save', even travel features look at 'How to have a holiday like me'. There is, of course, a subsection to this genre – the 'How not to...' article, which looks at how not to do whatever the writer is warning about, from personal experience or otherwise.

Inspirational

In which the reader is urged to go out and achieve something, be it follow a recipe, run a marathon, start a business, use a new lipstick, find love, stand for office, do their tax return, etc. Often combined with a how to feature or a case study based feature.

Warning

The opposite of the inspirational feature, in which the reader is warned against doing something – for example, don't marry your first love, never wear yellow, don't get wrinkles, do not let your adult children live with you, etc.

The explainer

In which the feature highlights a mystery and attempts to solve it, or is an expose of some kind, or thinks there is something that happened in the past (either historically or in the recent past) that you need to know about. For example, 'Where is Lord Lucan?', 'What really killed off the dinosaurs?', 'Everything you need to know about World War One', etc.

A straight feature

A feature that seeks to explore a particular angle of a subject using a combination of techniques, such as case studies, expert opinion, reportage, interviews, etc., in continuous prose. Could also be called a multi-source feature.

Investigative feature

A feature where the journalist has used a variety of reporting techniques to find information that isn't readily available, often to expose wrongdoing.

Self-help or personal improvement piece

A feature that aims to help you improve your own life, be it in emotional, physical, financial or other terms. Of course, some features are a mixture of the above genres. You might get a how to feature which is also something of a personal reflective essay or self-help feature, or a news feature written in list form, or any other combination.

Not every subject can be written about in every way but many subjects do work in more than one way, meaning that you can often use your research for one article to then write a significantly different article in another genre for another publication.

Let's take the Ebola virus, which at the time of writing this book is a major news story. You might write a warning article, in which you tell your readers what might happen when the disease spreads. You might write a 'how to' piece, be it how to avoid Ebola or what to do if you come into contact with it. You might write an explainer piece looking at what exactly Ebola is and how it spreads. Or a reportage piece on how hospitals are preparing for potential Ebola cases. Or case study pieces from people who have survived Ebola or relatives of people who have died from it. Or a look at other viruses that have spread around the world written in list form. Or you might go back and do a historical explainer piece looking at what happened to other viruses, such as avian flu and SARS.

Task: Type of feature

Have a look at the features in several publications. Try to work out what kind of feature each one is. You may want to use my categories, or to make up descriptions yourself.

Feature	Type

What is a feature idea?

Many people make the mistake of thinking a feature idea is just a subject, but actually the subject is just the beginning. An idea is what happens when you consider a particular aspect of a subject (known as the angle) and think about it with a specific audience in mind.

You can think of this in terms of an equation, or formula:

Feature idea = subject + angle + audience

If any one of these changes, then you have a new idea.

Later on in this book we will expand this so that the equation has an extra component:

Idea = (subject + angle + audience) + hook

But for now, ignore the hook.

Let's look at each of these components in turn.

Subject

This is the overarching area your idea falls into. Football, for example, or guitars or jam or leggings or Kenya. Note that the subject is not as broad as sport, music, food, clothes or Africa, but goes down a level from that.

Angle

This is the aspect of the subject you are looking at. Take jam, for example. Your angle may be how to make it or how to eat it or how to store it or regional differences or its history or best flavour combinations or removing jam stains or the price of jam or any one of a huge number of angles. It should never be 'here is everything you need to know about jam'.

Audience

This is who you are writing your article for and can be as broad as an age group (over sixties, kids, thirty-somethings, etc.), a job type (farmers, chefs, waiters, students, etc.) or another defining feature (diabetics, middle classes, Londoners, home cooks, etc.).

Change any one of these and you get a completely new idea. For example:

- An article on how to make jam, written for diabetics
- An article on how to make jam, written for kids
- An article on how to make jam, written for people who live in a hot country
- An article on how to eat jam, written for people who live in a hot country
- An article on how to eat jam, written for people allergic to wheat (no scones!)
- An article on how to eat chutney, written for people allergic to wheat (no sandwiches!).

They are all completely different articles.

It may be easier to see this in table form:

Subject	Angle	Audience
Jam	How to make it	Diabetics
Jam	How to make it	Kids
Jam	How to make it	People who live in a hot country
Jam	How to eat it	People who live in a hot country
Jam	How to eat it	People allergic to wheat
Chutney	How to eat it	People allergic to wheat

The same rule applies however 'serious' a subject you are writing about. If, for example, you are writing about child mortality, your table might look like this:

Subject	Angle	Audience
Maternal mortality rates	Avoidable maternal deaths in UK hospitals	Midwives
Maternal mortality rates	Avoidable maternal deaths in UK hospitals	Parents to be
Maternal mortality rates	Lessons we can learn from a country with a lower maternal mortality rate	Midwives
Stillbirth rates	Lessons we can learn from a country with a lower mortality rate	Midwives
Stillbirth rates	Lessons we can learn from a country with a lower mortality rate	Parents to be
Stillbirth rates	What happens after a still birth in terms of legal processes, e.g. maternity leave, registering the birth and death, etc.	Parents to be

Of course, once you have worked out who your audience is, you need to determine which publications they read. In practice, as a freelance journalist you often work out which publication you are targeting first and then think about your audience. If you work in-house then you will already know the answer to this, although different sections of your publication may have different readerships, of course.

Although it is tempting to think that all publications on the same subject have a similar audience, this is not the case. No two publications have exactly the same readership, although sometimes there is a crossover or 'floating readers' who do not have loyalty to any specific publication. This applies to newspapers, magazines and websites. It is easy to tell the difference when it comes to newspapers. For example, in the UK the *Guardian* and the *Telegraph* are both serious newspapers, but have different political leanings. Sometimes it is harder to discern when it comes to magazines. It often comes down to the demographic of the reader – how old they are, what class they belong to, where they live, what job they do, what their aspirations are. A good example would be to look at food magazines. In the UK, *Waitrose Kitchen*, *BBC Good Food*, *Olive*, *Delicious* and *Sainsbury's Magazine* are all very different.

You need to have an idea of who the reader is in order to be able to judge whether your article is appropriate for them. For example, you probably wouldn't write a piece on eating roadkill for a magazine whose readership is mostly urban, or if you did you would have to acknowledge this in your piece and tailor it accordingly, perhaps looking at urban roadkill, such as pigeons, squirrels and foxes.

The best way to understand a publication is to spend some time looking at the advertisements. Companies do not spend a lot of money trying to reach people who will never buy their products. By looking at the advertisements you can build up a picture of who the readers are, what they buy and what they aspire to buy. Of course, reading the publication helps enormously too.

When thinking about your audience, and how an article might work for them, think about an expert and then work down. For example, a chef would know more than an enthusiastic amateur. An enthusiastic amateur would know more than someone who dabbles in cooking.

Tip: Everything is interesting

There is no such thing as a highbrow object or lowbrow object. Think about lipstick. In some articles it may just represent make-up, as in what is the best make-up to wear for a certain scenario. In another it may be the starting point for an article about animal testing. It may be used as a symbol of female repression or emancipation or an analysis of chemical production or an indicator of economic success. Do not be bound by your initial impressions of an object – think around it.

Task: Identify the audience

Go to a good newsagent that doesn't mind you spending time browsing and look at all the publications available. Where there are subjects with many publications on a similar theme try to work out the differences between their audiences.

Publication title	Audience description

Task: Write a pen portrait

Look carefully through a publication. Taking in all of the articles, and all of the adverts, see if you can write a pen portrait of a typical reader, which is where you draw a picture of someone using words; that is, your description brings them to life. The following questions might help:

- What age range are they?
- Are they male or female?
- How well educated are they?
- How much do they earn?
- What is their household income?
- What are their hobbies?
- What do they do for work?
- What do they like to eat for dinner?
- What do they wear when they are getting dressed up?
- Where do they go on holiday?
- What snacks do they eat?
- How much do they spend on groceries?

(Continued)

(Continued)

- What do they watch on television?
- What exercise do they do?
- How often do they have sex and who with?
- What is the last book they read?
- What film would they see if they went to the cinema tonight?
- What is their house like?
- Who are their friends?

Once you have an idea of the reader you get an idea of what they may want to read.

When coming up with a feature idea, you can begin with the subject, the angle or the audience. It may be that you are thinking about a subject and decide it is something you want to write about. Perhaps you find synchronised swimming fascinating and would like the opportunity to find out more about it. If this is the case you would then need to do some research to help you come up with a specific angle for a feature on synchronized swimming. Or you may start with an angle – perhaps you have heard of several schools setting up synchronized swimming clubs and want to investigate the reasons for this trend. Or you may start with an audience and try to think about what they may like, or need, to read – in this case perhaps it would be PE teachers. It doesn't matter where your idea originates, but before you consider pitching it, let alone start writing it, you will need to be able to identify the subject, angle and audience. Without all of those you do not have an idea.

Task: Identify the subject, angle and audience

Look through a publication and identify the subject, angle and audience for each feature. (It may be that the audience is all readers of that publication. But the audience may be a subsection of the readership, such as teachers, women or sports fans or even women teachers who are sports fans.)

Subject	Angle	Audience

Defining audiences

It can be helpful to have a list, either physical or in your head, of types of audience. This means that when you come up with an angle and a subject you can easily work through a list of audiences to see which ones will match that subject and angle. Once you get used to doing this you can often sell very similar ideas to different publications – and because the audience is different, the tone, language, examples and interviewees will also be different.

Task: Types of audience

Write a list of types of audience that you can apply to subjects and angles. I have started you off with ten. Try to add at least ten more.

1 Married people
2 Single people
3 Straight people
4 Gay people
5 Retired people
6 People with young children
7 Teenagers
8 Members of the military
9 Unemployed people
10 Healthcare professionals
11 _____
12 _____
13 _____
14 _____
15 _____
16 _____

(Continued)

(Continued)

17 _____

18 _____

19 _____

20 _____

Now try to come up with more specialised groups of people that combine two characteristics – for example, they are a home cook and they own an AGA, or they are an amputee and they enjoy extreme sports. These are the articles you can sell to specialist publications.

I have started you off with five. Try to add another five:

1   Home cooks who have an AGA
2   Amputees who enjoy extreme sports
3   Female football fans
4   Aid workers in Africa
5   Parents of disabled children
6   _____
7   _____
8   _____
9   _____
10 _____

2 Getting ideas from objects

A good 'ideas person' should be able to take any object from their bag, be it a pen or a sweet, a tampon or a condom, a torch or a penknife, and use it as inspiration for several feature articles.

For example, at a basic level you could ask questions such as what the object is made of, where is it from and who makes it. This may lead to features about the child labourers making your pen or the remote village whose economy relies on you buying sweets. It might pose questions such as the impact on the local economy of wherever your pen is made if people stop buying pens, or if eating sweets goes completely out of fashion. Maybe there is an article in the journey your pen takes from the factory to your bag, or how many air miles there are in your sweets.

You might also ask questions about the object in relation to a group of people. Not all group/object pairings will yield ideas but many will. Perhaps there is a type of sweet that all soldiers eat to give them energy or boost their morale or because they are given them for free or because they are considered to be a patriotic type of sweet. Perhaps, thinking about sweets and old people, there is an article about the impact of certain sweets on false teeth, or the nostalgia certain sweets evoke. An article about how to make vegetarian sweets may occur to you or the ideal sweets to get new parents through the early days of exhaustion with a newborn. Or back to vegetarians and thinking about pens, perhaps you may think about squid ink or animal products used in processing plastic and come up with the idea of looking at everyday objects that contain animal products and how vegetarians (or, more likely, vegans) deal with this.

As you get used to using this technique, you will start to develop your own list of questions about each object, and any object can be inspiring providing you look at that object and ask yourself the right questions.

Here are some of the questions I ask myself about any object:

- Who made it? What is it made from? Are the materials rare? How are the materials created? Does it have an environmental impact? Is anyone exploited in getting these materials? What is the raw cost of the material? Where is it made?

- Is it fashionable? What is the most expensive version of the object? What is the cheapest version of the object? Where can you buy it? How would you feel if you were given one as a present? Is it beautiful?
- Do people use it differently according to their age? Do people use it differently according to their gender? Is it used differently in other parts of the world? Will future generations have them? Did past generations have them? What is its history? Is it cool? Is it accessible to everyone?
- Is it disposable? Is it recyclable? How many does the average person own? Are there variations of the product, e.g. different colours? Could we live without it?
- What other uses are there for the object, other than its obvious use? Is it commonplace to own one? What would you think of someone who didn't own one? When was the last time you used one? What would it happen if it disappeared?

I then applied these questions to a biro I took from my bag. Thinking about my pen in this way sparked many feature ideas, some by directly thinking about the pen, some by allowing my thinking to go off at tangents. These include:

1 Ten cool pens.
2 Why are newspaper letters editors suspicious of green ink?
3 What does your pen say about you?
4 Whether you really can use a biro to perform a tracheotomy and other examples of household objects used to save lives.
5 How to make your own pen from scratch.
6 In the age of computers, do pens have a future?
7 The town that makes the world's pens (if indeed there is a centre of industry).
8 How to prevent your pen causing a callous on your finger.
9 The people who still use fountain pens.
10 People who have used the same pen their whole life.

Some ideas you have in this way won't work as features. But, if you come up with many ideas, some of them will work. As you do this more and more you will get a feel for which ones to let go and which ones to pursue.

Remember, in this example the pen is the subject. The above list is the angle. But you still need an audience before these are full ideas.

Don't believe this process can work for anything? For this example I delved into my bag and pulled out a tampon. And I was able to come up with ten ideas very quickly. I have added in a potential audience here to give more of an idea about how these features might work (remembering that many of your feature ideas will never make it to pitch stage). As you will see, some are essentially the same idea as the pen, just substituting tampon for pen.

1 The different types of tampon with pros and cons (teenage girls).
2 What do women without access to sanitary protection use (general interest)?
3 The environmental impact of tampon use (general interest).
4 Types of sanitary protection including new developments, and how we need to be open to trying new methods as we get older (women in their thirties).
5 How to make your own tampons and sanitary towels (environment pages).
6 How the mooncup (a type of reusable internal blood catcher) was invented (business pages).
7 The town that makes the world's tampons (if indeed there is a centre of industry).
8 The changing face of tampon and sanitary towel advertising (for people working in advertising).
9 The changing face of tampon and sanitary towel advertising (for women's pages/general interest).
10 Real men buy tampons – things your partner may ask you to do and what you need to know to do this properly (twenty-something men).

Task: Ideas from objects

Take an object at random from your bag or desk. Ask yourself as many questions about it as you can think of. Use these to generate some potential feature ideas. See if you can get to ten.

1 _____
2 _____
3 _____
4 _____
5 _____
6 _____
7 _____
8 _____
9 _____
10 _____

My story – Emily Jupp

Emily Jupp is a freelance feature writer.

I had been on a Jane Austen parade with my friend – it's a parade that happens every year in the city of Bath, and everyone dresses up in Regency costume including bonnets. I really wanted to write something on it but it just wasn't the right time as it was a year too early for the 200th anniversary of

(Continued)

(Continued)

Pride and Prejudice being published which would have been an ideal hook. But I still really wanted to do something on Jane Austen and how I thought she was very good at dealing with matters of the heart and didn't really believe in marrying for money, which was quite a trailblazing idea at the time, and then I was sent some information about a book due to be published which was a reworking of the dating book *The Rules*, but saying that you should live your love life the way Jane Austen set out in her letters and her novels.

So, instead of just writing about the book I thought about all the dressing up and the experience on the parade and thought that maybe I could live by the rules of the book for a feature. The rules were about your romantic life but also about the way you handle yourself in your normal life. It was just meant to be a silly thing really but it did make me think about the importance of having a belief system and sticking to it and showing it through your actions rather than chatting about what you think but not really living by it. The rules were things like wearing appropriate attire and speaking up when you have a different opinion instead of ignoring it for the sake of social niceties. It all fell apart when my friend had a hot tub party and I knew Jane Austen wouldn't have approved of it but I went anyway.

The piece ran as a 1,300 word feature in the *Independent* with pictures of me in my Regency gown. I got a lot of nice comments on it. Off the back of that, every so often I get sent Jane Austen things or asked 'Would you like to try living like x?' – but nothing else has tempted me yet.

Tip: Follow the money

It can be handy, both in coming up with ideas and in researching your ideas, to question who is funding whatever you are writing about, be it the production of a new object, an arts performance, a public health campaign or anything else. Trying to answer the question is a good discipline to develop and can lead to interesting angles.

My story – Michael Cross

Michael Cross is news editor of the *Law Society Gazette*.

I wrote an article about what happened to the solicitors who joined the armed forces in the first month of the First World War. We were launching a new website to mark its centenary and quickly needed some material to post in it. I also wanted to encourage readers to contribute material, so needed to run something quickly that would spark their interest. I only really had a couple of hours of research time so I had to start with material that I knew was there, so I started with the back editions of the *Law Society Gazette*. I knew that 100 years ago every edition ran a list of the gentleman who became solicitors. So I had the names and ages of everyone who became a solicitor in August 1914. I also had the book of the Record of Service containing details of every solicitor who was in the armed forces. So by cross-checking from one to the other I was able to identify which of the 17 solicitors on the list had fought in the war. Of them, nine had gone into the forces. Six of the nine were casualties and three were killed. This produced a really nice snapshot. If, when doing the research, I had found it was a particularly lucky group, I'd have picked another month to look at so in that respect I had to keep an open mind but the results fitted in roughly with what I was expecting – the death rate among solicitors was about twice that of other people who went into the army. This is because they mostly went in as junior officers in the infantry, and this was the most dangerous job. The article was a nice way of giving an introduction to what solicitors did in that war, was relevant to our readership and would encourage people to come up with stories from their own families and firms.

When you need to find something new around a particular angle, the crucial thing is to know what raw material is out there and base your research around that. I had to think of a way to combine what was readily available into a short feature that hopefully a lot of people would read. The danger with doing this sort of feature is that there are always more things you can look up, For example, I was able to find details about the families of the people who were killed. You have to stick to what you need to go in the feature, and double check when you can. Also, it's quite possible the original source got something wrong so you need to double check all the available information. The whole thing took about three hours.

The subject has so many potential features. I am interested in the Inns of Court Battalion, which was an Officer Training Corps and that still exists as a regiment. I'm very keen to cover not just the people who were killed – in a sense they are the easy ones to find out about, but what happened to those who were disabled or who came through without a scratch. I'm very interested in officers who were Court Martial Officers. You might have been an articled clerk specialising in conveyancing and be volunteered to be a defending solicitor in a court martial. The danger is to go off into the wealth of information out there. It's great if you are a historian and being paid to find out the whole archive but the journalist needs to know what they need to know and know what material is available. So what I've also done is get a couple of other volunteers and amateur historians doing some of the legwork for me. One is a guy who collects medals from the First World War.

(Continued)

(Continued)

He's been collecting material about individual soldiers for 50 years so he can remember off the top of his head the life story of everyone who won a Victoria Cross, for example. He's keen to contribute because he's a solicitor. It's really useful to find people like that. And whenever he comes to London, I buy him a beer.

Task: Connect unconnected ideas

Choose two seemingly unconnected ideas and objects and see whether you can come up with any links between them. For example, wedding rings and USB sticks, stay-at-home dads and plastic bags, bottled water and bogeys. Do any ideas come from these? Already I am thinking about the health risks posed by drinking from bottles that people have touched on the supermarket shelves and wondering how long germs can live in the open air. Also, the environmental impact of stay-at-home parents (e.g. more packaging for packed lunches on daytrips) and also tips for buying jewellery over the internet.

3 The Lego example

As explained in the previous chapter, any object or subject should lead to multiple feature ideas. As an example I have chosen the toy Lego.

I am currently interested in Lego because my children have just got to the age where they enjoy playing with Lego. In addition to this, my parents have just unearthed a box of Lego they saved from my childhood and given it to my children to play with and we have been asked to take my husband's childhood Lego out of his parents' loft.

Practically without thinking about it, the following ideas popped into my head while writing the above paragraph:

- Which toys work across the generations and what is it that makes them last in this way?
- Conversely, which toys were very popular at various points in history and didn't stand the test of time?
- Does plastic last forever? Is it safe to use old plastic toys? How should you clean plastic toys stored in the loft?
- An audit of people's lofts.
- Who is better at Lego, a three-year-old (my daughter) or a 33-year-old (my husband) – give them challenges in Lego and look at how they approach these.

Of course, every person has different ideas and different frames of reference. An excellent way to get fresh ideas is just to ask people for them.

To prove this, first I emailed some journalist friends and asked them to tell me, off the top of their heads, what feature ideas came to them when thinking about Lego. I got the following responses:

> I think the most interesting thing about Lego concerns Lego and feminism. I would peg it in terms of the advert from ages ago that went viral of a girl with red hair playing with it, that everyone was comparing to ads nowadays. I think they are going back to doing things to make the product more inclusive and non-gendered so would go with that to

make a feature about the evolution of Lego and lessons about feminism. The title would be 'What Lego tells us about the feminist movement'.

Something maybe for *Psychologies* or a parenting magazine about imaginative play and how Lego's focus on 'sets' that have instructions and can only be built one way have had an impact on kids' imaginative play. For my generation, Lego was a springboard to creative and imaginative construction but now it seems to be a lesson in consumerism as kids just crave set after set.

First thing that comes to mind is the genderisation of Lego – you know, that 1981 ad with a little girl in dungarees and pigtails showing her Lego construction, compared with a more recent ad showing some very gendered pink stuff. And the whole Lego women scientist figure thing where it turned out it was just a media stunt and they only made a few!

Something around the science of toy mash-ups. What's that ability children have to dismantle, break, scrawl over, behead and generally mash-up their pristine toys (which are pristine for maybe five minutes) into something which actually is better but bears no resemblance whatsoever to the neat and sensible playing on the advert? Where does it come from? And why do we lose it? Maybe on the anniversary of the first *Toy Story* film which had amazing crazed weird toy creations.

Has Lego become too expensive? A piece looking at rising and often extortionate prices of some sets. With examples and anecdotes.

Is Lego addictive? One mum in the playground this morning said she didn't mind that it rained during her week in France this summer as the children played Lego all day. It's not just the Lego itself but the endless YouTube videos etc. that go with it. Basically, a look at the debate on whether Lego is always good or whether it has a more sinister side (antisocial, etc?).

When did Lego become more than just child's play? I'd probably look into Lego art and architecture and write about the artists that work with it and why they choose it as their medium above all else. Maybe a bit about how Lego has evolved as a brand so it's not all about kids.

How Lego helps develop children's brains for something like *School Report* or *Mother & Baby*.

Five entrepreneurs whose love of Lego led to success – for the trade press and newspapers.

'My son didn't speak – but Lego opened up our path to communication' for a family section of a newspaper.

How about a feature on how the way you keep your Lego bricks defines you? Are you a meticulous sorter or do you dump the lot in a big box? Will sorters make great managers, will dumpers to be disorganised people who never finish projects? Talk to famous people and ask if they were sorters or dumpers and see how they worked out.

And, from a friend of mine who is an editor on the *Financial Times*:

Earlier this year I commissioned and edited a piece on the revival of Lego, from a company facing bankruptcy ten years ago to the world's most profitable toy company today. It was written by Richard Milne, our Nordic correspondent. Apart from being a great business turna-round story, we thought our readers would feel nostalgic about playing with Lego and probably bought it for their kids now. We published it as *The Lego Movie* hit the cinemas, so was good timing.

I then I emailed non-journalist friends, asking them what they thought of when it came to Lego, in terms of what they would like to read more about, and got these responses:

One thing to consider is the massive proliferation of Lego-based anima-tion and computer games. It is my suspicion that their huge popularity has had an impact on the continuing popularity of traditional Lego – as well as on the making of the successful film.

I've always been intrigued about what motivates people who make huge or unusual things with it – there is a life-size naked man made of Lego in the window of the Condomerie in Amsterdam. We stay at the Headland Hotel in Cornwall every year with my girlfriend's family (where the film adaptation of Roald Dahl's *The Witches* was filmed) – they have a huge Lego model of the hotel that was made by a guest.

When and why they chose to have coloured faces and a look at the toys becoming racially defined. Whether it is true or a myth that the market-ing was unisex in the 1970s and 1980s. Do other countries have different colour bricks and why it was just red, yellow, green, blue?

My mum and I were talking about it recently and she said that with my brother they sometimes got sets that were too old for him and therefore too complex – and one year my dad spent weeks setting up a pirate galleon ship with loads of fiddly bits while my brother played with other toys.

I love Lego. I have always loved Lego. I have boxes and boxes of Technic Lego from my childhood and intend to get my children into it as soon as possible. They are already keen Duplo builders. My main unanswered questions about Lego are how do they design and test models and how do they decide what models to take to final develop-ment and retail, and also why would anyone ever want to build things that aren't Technic Lego? Surely you want to play with it, so it has to do things. I find the static models deeply unsatisfying on completion.

Why did Lego take off but Meccano has largely has fallen away?

Why doesn't Denmark's biggest export feature in *Borgen* or *The Killing*?

How children of different ages can all use Lego. Works with any age once they're past the stage of trying to eat it.

How do you get a job as a model builder at Legoland or even at the Lego Shop? What are the skills in the job description/person spec?

How many countries in the world have Lego? Is it different in different places? So can you get the bits for a Lego igloo in Greenland or the Taj Mahal in India?

Whenever I think of Lego I think of all the Lego my grandad bought for my boy cousins and how unfair it was he bought me none!

We are quite into Lego here. The main question that I would pose based on Lego would be to do with the choice to genderise it, so that there is 'normal Lego', which you can build anything from, in a whole range of primary/secondary/tertiary colours, and then 'girls' Lego' in pinks and purples. Is the Lego company driving this, or was it a response to customer demand? Also, the Lego Friends branding for girls versus the menacing characters aimed at boys (robbers, etc.). When did this begin? Is this a movement for the brand away from pure construction (some of the packs require little assembly, and are more like toys based on the theme than the original purpose of Lego) and towards a character-based narrative?

My massive thing about Lego is that it is very gendered. For girls there is Lego Friends which has women with shapes and is all about things like having a pony or shops or gardens. Then all the boy stuff is dragons and soldiers and castles and superheroes, which my daughter just wouldn't like. I looked for something for her that was in the middle and couldn't find anything.

Now it so happens that I am at an age where many of my friends have young children and we are thinking about Lego a lot. And, of course, I am sure I have particularly interesting and thoughtful friends – that's why I chose them (or why they chose me!). Even so, I think that if you ask any group of people about any subject you will get a range of interesting thoughts and ideas. And if the answer is 'I've never thought about that' you can ask them why not and see where that leads.

In fact, two friends went even further and sent me long replies about Lego.

This is from my friend David:

> Michael Chabon (*The Amazing Adventures of Kavalier and Clay*, *Wonder Boys*, *The Yiddish Policemen's Union*, etc.) writes about Lego in *Manhood for Amateurs*, a collection of essays on fatherhood, masculinity, etc. Actually, he writes about 'Legos', because he's an American and they get these things wrong.
>
> Here he is summing up the essay in question, 'To the LEGOland Station', talking about predetermined *Star Wars* play sets:
>
> '…inevitably, over time, the things kind of crumble and get destroyed and fall apart and then, once they do, the kids take all those pieces, and they create these bizarre, freak hybrids… Lego-things all getting mashed up together into this post-modern Lego stew… despite the best efforts of corporate retail marketing.'
>
> My own experience of reconnecting with Lego was initially a nostalgia for the old simple restrictions: the limited four- or five-colour palette, the uni-directional building options, the simplicity of the pieces that seemed to demand more imagination from the child. I was also disappointed that so many modern kits were based on battles, conflict, weaponry. There was even a recent study that showed how many more angry faces there were in Lego.
>
> Then I became more of an AFOL (Adult Fan of Lego), looking at ludicrously priced collectors' models from the various licensed franchises (*Lord of the Rings*, *Star Wars* – even *Indiana Jones*, *Ghostbusters* and *Back To The Future* – which shows you just who these sets are aimed at). I am still disheartened that Lego boxes no longer include suggestions for other things to build with the bits in the box, the way the sets I remember always did. Instead, they make a feature of any model that is '2 in 1' or '3 in 1' and are again prescriptive about the other builds available. All Lego is, of course, 'infinity in 1', but that suggests you may not need any more of the stuff, so the angle is never pushed.
>
> *The Lego Movie* takes all this tension at the heart of Lego as its theme. The movie is about the different ways of playing with or collecting Lego. There are the free spirits (like the ginger girl in the 1970s Lego ad that was shared on social media recently: 'What it is is beautiful'), known in the film as Master Builders, who can see the infinite possibilities in combinations of bricks. And there are the obedient construction workers who always follow the instructions and are distrustful or downright hostile to anything that isn't constructed according to the rules. The baddie is Lord Business, who wants to stick everything in place so it can never be changed and remains in its 'correct' form. The real-world equivalents – who make it into the film in a really extraordinary sequence that I won't

spoil if you haven't seen it – are the AFOL, who buys expensive sets, assembles them once and puts them on a shelf never to be played with or mixed up with other sets and built into new creations, and the imaginative, creative child, who plays with Lego, creates a narrative and enjoys juxtaposing pieces from different themes to create something new (or just flat out doesn't care what 'belongs' with what).

Of course, the movie (and its merchandising) has it both ways. Master Builders are supposedly encouraged to be creative via new sets that – surprise! – make more than one model, though simply including step-by-step instructions for more than one thing is just as prescriptive in my opinion. And AFOLs get to marvel at the extraordinary new sets and their even more extraordinary price tags. *The Lego Movie* has its cake and eats it, and then gets everybody to buy even more cake as soon as they leave the cinema.

Then there's the gender angle – one Lego catalogue we received had a separate Lego Friends pull-out, implying that all the other sets were for boys. And, in fact, almost all the other sets were licensed conflict-based kits with almost no female mini figures.

I realise all this is not really what you asked for, but it's definitely what I think about when I think about Lego...

And from my friend Rob:

Something that I would like to look at myself from a purely parenting perspective is how many children actively played with Lego and made models from their own imaginations (Master Builders) before going on to a university course in a creative subject (including Engineering, Graphics, Art/Sculpture, etc.) and subsequently building a successful career in their degree-related subject?

If there is correlation in this, a more detailed look at what they built compared to what they make now could be interesting i.e. did those who built houses or skyscrapers go on to be civil or structural engineers or did those who built aircraft or rockets go on to be aerospace engineers.

The thing I find disturbing about Lego is that they have the patent for all different types of Lego bricks, that is bricks that lock together to build complex structures. This essentially gives them the monopoly on this kind of toy. This, to me, is one of the reasons why Lego is so expensive – they have the market cornered.

The cool part of it now is the advent of computer games and virtual worlds where Minecraft essentially takes the concept of Lego and applies it to a virtual world, where users can build cityscapes to sheer randomness to their hearts' content. Lego, I think, missed a trick here (unless they own Minecraft) as their computer games failed to take advantage of this early on. Furthermore, with the release of *The Lego Movie* the toy maker has pushed its reach further into the lives of children where Lego is no longer just in the toy room causing parents anguish as it buries its eight nobbly bits into the bridge of their foot or causing children anguish as they watch a bit disappear up the vacuum cleaner, it's now on the TV and in computer game consoles.

This is also slightly worrying as, even though it's still a family business (as far as I'm aware), the behemoth of a company is becoming ever more influential. It's partnership with Shell or genderisation of models is, to me, of particular concern as it holds such sway over a child's development. I would compare it to a Cbeebies cartoon showing the exploitation of the planet or a 1960s style cartoon of a family home with the mum only there to look pretty and cook for her breadwinner man.

What's also interesting is the Lego house built by James May in his 'Toy Stories' show. As a two-storey house it was worth next to nothing but as a piece of art it was worth a small fortune. I would also hope that, in terms of degradable characteristics, Lego would not or should not be degradable over any short-term period. It should be (and can be) easily recycled, either by selling it on, or shredding it to use as plastic infill. Lego has no moving parts and is very robust, which goes against the grain of our very consumerist society. Broken Lego bricks could continue be used for a different purpose in the Lego world or should find their way into the recycling.

I feel the mini figure and bespoke parts for specific models is moving against the principles in which the Lego brick was created. It is meant to exercise a child's imagination and with some of the bespoke bricks, this is stifled by the fact that the brick/part cannot be used in any other way other than as specified in the instructions. Older kits came with two or even three models that could be built with the parts. One kit of mine could make a fire engine or a 4×4 with a trailer and fireboat. Another built a moon buggy or a submarine. The kits now don't give you this option which I feel is a big loss as it removes choice from the child.

As for the friend who said she was completely uninspired by this subject, well that led to an idea about kids who don't get into or have access to popular toys.

It took just a few minutes to send an email to friends and colleagues asking for their current thoughts on Lego. As you can see, the ideas that came back from them could lead to a huge number of ideas and, hopefully, commissions. Of course, your friends might get bored if you ask them to do your work for you every week, but you don't have to explicitly send out requests for them to do your thinking for you. Just talk to anyone about any subject in the pub or over coffee or when you bump into them. Some of these conversations will lead to ideas.

After I asked my friends and colleagues about their Lego ideas, I looked up some of the features that have been written about Lego. Here are just ten I picked from many more:

1 The *BBC Magazine* did a feature on the theoretical height that a Lego tower could get to before the bricks buckled under the weight.
2 Also in the *BBC Magazine* was this story (in 2014) about the Cornish beach where pieces of Lego still wash up after a cargo ship carrying Lego had an accident in 1997.
3 The fashion blog of the *Guardian* ran a short piece about ways it had found to wear Lego, first looking at a Chanel handbag based on a Lego brick and also mentioning various items of Lego-based jewellery.
4 Art critic Jonathan Jones wrote a blog for the *Guardian* on whether Lego can be considered art.
5 The *Independent* celebrated 50 years of Lego by giving a bucketful of bricks to various celebrities, talking to them about their memories of Lego and seeing what they would build with it.
6 The *Daily Mail* ran a feature about a couple, Craig McCartney and Lindsey Haggerty, from Scotland, who are travelling around the world and who take pictures of Lego mini figures representing themselves in every place they go. These are the basis for a Facebook page with thousands of followers.
7 The *Daily Express* published a feature about adults who make a living making bespoke Lego models, such as 43-year-old Duncan Titmarsh, who left his job as a kitchen fitter to start a company called Bright Bricks, creating Lego models for commercial and private clients, and running Lego building events, workshops and parties. 'Prices for a bespoke creation range from around £80 to £40,000 and his workshop houses around nine million bricks.'
8 www.salon.com ran a feature about an American twelve-year-old, Shubham Banerjee, who built a Braille printer out of a Lego Mindstorms kit. The printer, which took four weeks and had seven failed prototypes before one that worked, cost about $350 compared to $2,000 for conventional Braille printers.
9 To tie in with the release of *The Lego Movie*, the *Daily Telegraph* went to the Lego headquarters in Bilund, Denmark and wrote a feature that is essentially a history of Lego and a look at how the toy has developed.
10 The *Sun* ran a story about a woman Harry Potter fan who made a replica of Hogwarts School out of 400,000 Lego bricks. The headline was: 'Mum Hogs the Lego to build huge replica of Harry Potter school'.

Task: Ask friends about objects

Choose any object. Ask your friends, family and colleagues for their thoughts on it. Ask them just to tell you what comes to mind initially, rather than spending too long on the subject. See what ideas stem from these conversations.

4 Getting ideas from your own life and the lives of your friends and family

My story – Kate Hilpern

Kate Hilpern is a freelance feature writer.

I'm adopted and when I was eighteen I looked for my biological family and I found that my birth mother had died in mysterious circumstances when she was nineteen, while travelling in India. I had then gone to India with my birth father in 1999 and discovered she was probably murdered. I'd written about it a little while after going, in a piece for *The Times*, but had to be particularly careful then because certain family members were still alive.

I'd been looking through some old letters that had belonged to my mother and it occurred to me that I often find it quite cathartic to write things down. I pitched it to one *Guardian* editor as a first-person case study piece for their 'Experience' slot but they said it wasn't right for that slot but it was a fascinating story and how about pitching it to the 'Family' section. I'd written for that section before so I called one of the editors I know and told him about it and said that because it was such a personal piece I wanted to be able to give it a go but to give it up if it wasn't working or if I decided I didn't want it published. He was very easy about this and left the whole thing up to me in terms of timing and direction.

I wrote it over a period of many weeks and kept going back to it. It was quite upsetting to write and I nearly gave up writing it. It was only when I started to tidy it up and turn it into a narrative that it started to feel cathartic. It was a 2,000-word feature in the end. Because I only know snippets about my birth mother and no one really talks her about much, it helped make her more real, if that makes sense. Knowing there are many other stories similar to hers, it also felt good to share her story in the hope that it might help others. It got over 2,000 shares on social media and lots of comments and the editor contacted me afterwards to say it had gone down very well online, which is often a hard thing to pull off.

I'm very mindful of things being online forever so when I write anything personal I try not to write anything that could upset or embarrass anyone involved in that story, either now or in the future. That is probably more relevant for when I write about my own children, which I don't do very often for that very reason. But in this case, I had my mother's surviving relatives at the front of my mind and was careful to take into account any feelings they could have about the feature, while at the same time balancing that consideration with the fact that this was my account of my own story and important to me.

You might not think that your own life is particularly interesting. Or you might have taken the stance that you don't want to do 'personal journalism' and want to keep your life and the lives of your friends and family separate from your journalism. That is fine, but it doesn't mean that you can't use their lives, and yours, as inspiration for articles that, once written, don't have any specific links back to the stories, circumstances and situations that inspired them.

Think about conversations you have had with friends recently. What issues have they brought up?

Some examples that occurred to me:

- A friend in her mid-thirties told me that she is worried about internet dating in case men think she is just looking for someone to father her children before it is too late.
- A friend told me they give their parents money every month to help them with bills and shopping.
- My friend's band has started to get airplay and gigs and looks on the verge of being a big success.
- A colleague was finding it hard to get a parents' evening appointment at her child's school that worked with her own work commitments.

And some things that have happened in my own life:

- I went out for dinner with my team at work so we could get to know each other, and the new members of staff, a bit better.
- We had our bathroom ripped out and a new one put in (and as I made the bathroom fitter a cup of coffee he told me about a previous job where the owner was around during the whole two weeks it took to do the job and didn't offer to make him a drink even once).
- I started to shop for my children's Christmas stocking presents.
- I went to stay at a friend's house for a weekend while she was away so I could do some editing on this book without the usual demands of my home life.

None of the above are particularly strange or unusual. People often talk about their parents or dating or work on their house. We often know about a friend on the verge of great things, be it being in a band or about to get a promotion at work. Parents all have stories about their child's school. But once you apply your feature writer's brain to the above, you can start to see how these everyday happenings and conversations can lead to all kinds of ideas.

From the list above, here are some of mine. Remember, I am not censoring them so you can get an accurate picture of the ideas that come, even if they are not all good enough to make the final cut:

- How to start internet dating – a guide for women in their thirties.
- Women who met their (male) partners towards the end of their fertility window and how they brought up the subject of babies and how long they waited until they started trying to conceive.
- Men who feel their biological clock is ticking.
- Dating when you have children – different approaches, e.g. a parent who kept it a secret, a parent who let their child choose dates for them online, etc.
- Adults who financially support their parents – case study based feature.
- Financially sensible ways to help your parents – a guide to the best way to do this.
- What to do if your parents depend on you too much (not just financially, also emotionally, etc.).
- Start planning for your old age now – guides for people at different ages, such as what you can do to plan for this if you are currently in your twenties, thirties, forties, fifties, etc.
- When success comes later in life – a look at people who saw career success in their thirties, forties or later, such as older performers or novelists or business people.
- 'My dad's famous' – what to do if your parent suddenly becomes famous.
- 'I've achieved my goals. Now what?' How to refresh your ambitions so you always have something to aim for (relevant whatever your ambition was, be it to have a hit single or to have children or to run a marathon, etc.).
- The working parent's guide to managing your child's school – how you can still have meetings with teachers, join the governing body, etc., even if you can't attend meetings during working hours.
- A guide for schools and headteachers on how to work alongside working parents so that they do not feel excluded.
- How to create a team feeling – ways in which you can work better as a team in the workplace.
- Applying workplace team-building skills to your home life.
- Keeping your distance – how not to overshare with colleagues.

- Getting the most from builders – how to work together to ensure they want to do their best for you and your home.
- Things to think about when planning a new bathroom (for example, the height of towel rails so kids can reach them).
- Ideas for Christmas stocking fillers – what should go in them? I have heard the ditty 'something to eat, something to read, something for fun, something you need'.
- Christmas stocking ideas for all budgets.
- Christmas stockings for grown ups – what could you put in them?
- Life swapping with friends – what happens if you move into your friend's house for a weekend? Does it make you want their life or be pleased you have yours? Find real life examples or people willing to do this as an experiment.

Getting ideas from friends doesn't just mean meeting them in person and asking them what is going on in their life. In fact, if you just do that you're likely to end up with no friends as people refuse to tell you anything in case it ends up in print. The best ideas from friends may be sparked by something they have said or done but each idea will mutate as you think about it so that by the time the idea is fully formed no one would recognize that it came from them.

Remember, the inspiration for an idea can be mundane – it doesn't mean the feature that comes from it will be. Ask your friends what they had for breakfast – this could prove as fruitful in terms of ideas as asking them how they met their partner or about an exotic holiday they have had.

My story – Linda Geddes

Linda Geddes is a freelance journalist and former features editor of *New Scientist*.

Five or six years ago my husband proposed to me and, as we were both science journalists, my editor, more as a joke than anything else, said maybe we could do an experiment at the wedding. At first I just thought, 'Haha, how funny' but then I started to think that would be rather fun and what we could do. So the first thing I thought of testing was stress and whether it is really true that weddings are the most stressful event in your life and thought that maybe we could test our stress levels. But often your first idea isn't your best idea, plus it is quite difficult to measure stress and to define what we mean by stress.

(Continued)

(Continued)

Then I just happened upon a blog by a neuroeconomist called Paul Zak, talking about one of his student's research looking at why people cry at sad movies. And he had found that the people who are the most upset by an emotional film are the ones who release more of a hormone called oxytocin, often known as the cuddle chemical. I started wondering whether the same thing underpinned why people cry at happy events like weddings. And so I sent Paul Zak an email asking that question and saying 'I'm getting married and would you like to test it' and to my surprise he emailed right back and said yes.

I pitched the idea to my editor, he thought it was a great idea and asked me to cost his flights and car hire and we also had to find a way of getting a centrifuge for spinning the blood to a remote wedding venue in Devon. We also had to work out how to take blood and where to get the syringes from and things like that but, fortunately, a couple of my friends are doctors and nurses and we recruited them to take the blood samples.

Obviously it was going to be a small sample size. It wasn't going to have all of the scientific checks and balances that you might have in a rigorous clinical trial, but at the very least we thought it would provide a great narrative for a feature about recent insights into the role of oxytocin in the human body.

We took blood samples from ourselves – the bride and groom – plus eleven particularly close family members and friends, before and after the wedding ceremony, and looked at changes in several hormones, including oxytocin. We found that, indeed, the wedding seemed to increase oxytocin levels, not just in the bride and groom but in many of those watching, particular close family members. The research provided a brilliant narrative and it also laid the foundations for a series of follow-up studies by Paul Zak measuring oxytocin in natural human settings, including rugby matches and a war dance in Papua New Guinea.

You may want to develop a list of questions that you apply to any emotional situation you think about. These might include:

- Is it different for men and women?
- What was it like for a previous generation?
- Does it change as you age?
- What to do when the emotion is no longer there.

Take the death of a friend, for example. If you apply the above questions you may get the following ideas:

- When a close friend died, Jack felt like x but Jill felt like y. Why is this?
- One hundred years ago we were expected to hide our emotions when we experienced the loss of a friend or relative. Today a public outpouring of grief is all but expected. Why?
- Jack, aged 100, lost his best friend when he was 18, but says nothing has ever hit him so hard as his neighbour dying last year. Why, 82 years later, is his experience of grief so different?
- When Jill's best friend died she felt nothing. Why was this?

My story – Jenny Wood

Jenny Wood is a freelance journalist and former features editor of *LOOK* magazine.

A couple of years ago, I had a baby. One of the new mums I met, Jo, already had a child – when she was just 26, she volunteered at a Russian orphanage, where she met and fell in love with a little disabled girl there, Marina. She spent the next two years adopting her. Despite having no legs beneath the knee, and only one arm, Marina now lived a normal life. Both she and Jo were amazing, and I knew their story deserved a wider audience.

However, as a friend, I wanted to make sure any interview appeared in the right kind of publication, and for the right reasons. Jo wanted to encourage people to adopt, and to consider adopting a child with a disability, so I needed to place the story somewhere where these aims were likely to be met, rather than in a publication that just wanted a sensational feature. We came up with *Red* magazine. Grown-up and full of thought-provoking articles, its readers are women in their thirties and forties – the right age to be interested in adoption, or at least to donate to a charity such as the Russian orphanage Jo still supported.

My pitch involved a few paragraphs summing up Jo's experience, along with – crucially – photographs of Marina in Russia and the UK. Thankfully, *Red* agreed the story was the perfect fit, and Jo and I worked together on writing a piece she was happy with. The feature made everyone cry (a good thing, believe me!) and raised a large sum of money for the orphanage.

Task: Ideas from recent conversations

Think of some recent conversations you have had with friends. What did they tell you about? Try to come up with some ideas inspired by those conversations.

Conversation	Idea
	1
	2
	3
	1
	2
	3
	1
	2
	3

Social media can be an excellent way to get ideas from your friends. Here is an example of some of the ideas that came to me on the train one morning while scrolling through the timeline of friends' updates on Facebook on my smartphone. They are rough ideas, not fully worked through, but show how even a quick glance at social media should lead to many ideas, some of which may become a feature with a little work.

Facebook update: a cousin has posted a happy first birthday message to the family dog, with a picture of it.

• Look into whether 'pet birthdays' are a trend and how they are celebrated – with presents, cakes, photo shoots?
• How to make a cake suitable for your pet to eat (and can humans also eat it?).
• Look at how having a pet has changed the lives of families, with case studies.

Facebook update: a travel blogger I follow has said: 'After three days in this beautiful place, we are back in Athens and there's watermelon waiting for us in the freezer.'

• What fruits can be eaten frozen?
• Ideas for using up watermelon.
• Sweet treats that aren't bad for you.
• Great ideas for self-catering holidays.

Facebook update: someone I used to go to college with has posted a picture of their arrival at Las Vegas, somewhere I know they have been before.

- Why return to a place when there is so much of the world to see?
- Is anywhere ever as good the second time (include case studies)?
- Las Vegas with kids – what to do in a city made for gambling when children can't gamble.
- The other side of Las Vegas – the ordinary people who live and work there.

Facebook update: a freelance colleague posted a picture of his second letter in the same publication that year.

- People who write letters to newspapers and magazines – why?
- Find prolific letter-writers and interview them?
- Talk to letters editors about how to get your letter noticed.

Facebook update: two people in my wider circle of friends have posted pictures of siblings who died, on what would have been their birthday.

- How do you tell new friends or partners about tragedies in the past? At what point do you bring it up?
- How to tell your children about relatives who have died.
- Adults who lost a sibling in childhood and the impact it has had on their lives.
- Losing a sibling – the impact that losing a sibling can have (on an adult or child) and ways of coping with this.

I am also a fan of the online scrapbook website, Pinterest. If, for example, you follow the Royal Mint, you could end up with lots of ideas based on coins and plenty of hooks as they frequently give advance notice of new coin designs, often marking anniversaries. Similarly, if I knew that a publication was looking for articles on creating a nursery on a budget for your baby, I could search for budget nursery ideas and see what other people had done, and take inspiration from this.

Websites, of course, go in and out of fashion and new ones are being developed all the time, and you will work out which ones are your favourites and fruitful for you.

Task: Ideas from social media updates

Look at a social media site of your choice. Choose some of the updates and see what ideas they give you for articles.

Social media update	Idea	
	1	
	2	
	3	
	1	
	2	
	3	
	1	
	2	
	3	

My story – Olivia Gordon

Olivia Gordon is a freelance features journalist.

My son was born premature and was in hospital in the neonatal unit for his first five months.

Once I went back to work I had two separate ideas. One was to write something about the neonatal unit experience and how amazing the doctors and nurses are and the other was to write about the fetal medicine surgery that my son had and the fact he had a form of surgery while still in the womb when he was diagnosed with a condition called hydrops, when I was 29 weeks pregnant.

I pitched the fetal medicine idea to *The Times*. I'd written for them before, but not for their magazine, and I pitched something along the lines of the fetal medicine aspect and the amazing work they do and the editor got back to me and said they were going to do their annual children's doctors issue and she thought this could work for that. She ended up wanting it to be more about my story and my experience, which wasn't what I initially intended but I was happy to do that though I still want to do something about other people's experiences at some point.

The article turned out to be our personal story. It had a bit of context and history about fetal medicine but was basically our personal story of fetal medicine and the neonatal unit. What that magazine does very well is present the story so that it looks amazing, and with amazing photography, so they managed to get all the main doctors and nurses who looked after my son and photographed us together with them.

I've been very reluctant to mine my own life for features but I have done it, maybe more than I wanted to. It helped me a lot when getting into journalism. I usually try not to write anything extremely personal but obviously this was a very personal piece and I specifically requested that they didn't have comments online under the article as the whole thing was too raw and personal to have comments, not just about appearance, which is often what nasty comments focus on, but I didn't even want people to comment on the experience at all.

Of course, there is some information I didn't put into the article, it's a selected cut of what happened. It's about my son and I bore in mind that this will be on the internet for his lifetime and I didn't want to write anything that he might not want to read when he's older.

I think that actually, when you go through an experience like this, you write it in your head before writing it. So by the time it came to write it, I sat down and let it pour out and two or three hours later it was done. One of the reasons I pitched it to *The Times* was because I felt the way I'd already conceptualised it in my head was the way it would fit in a publication like that – I wouldn't have pitched it anywhere where I would have had to change my own voice.

I know that the doctors in the piece got a good response to it. I saw some recently and they said people talk to them about the article. Everyone was very, very helpful – and I did quite a long interview with the clinical director of the Fetal Medicine Unit who gave me a lot of history and context, which was helpful because my editor wanted more detail on this when she saw my initial draft. She also wanted more about certain aspects that I didn't think were important, such as why we'd gone ahead with the fetal surgery. For me, we just did it because doctors told us we should, so I had to state that more clearly.

I donated my fee to the Neonatal Unit and Fetal Medicine Unit. It was really my way of thanking them.

Every person you know, however much you rate their intelligence or think they have something interesting to say, is a mine of feature ideas. Sometimes, as we have seen, this can be unintentional. You may take inspiration from something they have said or done or told you about and write it in such a way that the person who inspired the original thought that sparked off the process would never even recognise themselves or their story in the finished piece. Sometimes, however, it pays to be open about looking for new ideas – after all, on the whole people enjoy being asked for their thoughts and ideas.

As an example, I emailed a selection of friends who do not work as journalists, told them I was thinking about new ideas for articles, and asked them the following questions:

1   What subject would you like to read more about right now?
2   What things are puzzling you right now?
3   Have you noticed any new trends recently?

Some of the responses I got back are given below.

What subject would you like to read more about right now?

I'd like to know more about gender-neutral parenting, how not to spend £100 a week at the supermarket, how to make new friends and how to look smart at work without being boring.

I'd like to read more about if there is a way of knowing the best time to book flights. If there's a guide to knowing with each airline if you're better off waiting until a few months or weeks beforehand, or booking a whole year in advance to get the best deal. Particularly on my mind at the moment, given we're going to visit my brother in Toronto next year and will have four return flights to pay for, ideally without having to re-mortgage!

I am really interested in knowing more about the background to the current news stories (as my history lessons at school were rubbish and I was forced to stop history at 14 to do cooking). For example, why are Israel and Gaza at war? Why is Scotland part of the UK? And so on.

I'd like to read more about women's rugby. In my newspaper this morning there were six pages of premiership football coverage about the first day of the season but just two paragraphs about England's women's rugby team winning the world cup.

I would like to read more about the benefits of immigration, to counter all the scaremongering that is rife in the papers.

I want to read more about the basic background of stories that have fully developed before I tune into them. For example, I hadn't heard of the Yazidi people until recently.

Men who work in childcare. Why aren't there more? You see plenty in Denmark and the Nordic countries.

Who are the people who believe what they read in the *Daily Mail*? Do they even know anyone from Romania? And are they aware they're being manipulated?

Who are all the people in my road, what do they do and what do their houses look like inside?

What I do read is a lot of articles about how climate change is dire, how no one who can take action will, and especially how all the scaremongering doesn't shake sense into the sceptics. We all just read things that increase our confirmation bias and basically the message is that we are all still screwed. Hurrah! What I would like to know about is, given all this, what can we do about it? If no one's mind can be changed, what now? How can we act positively? How can the environmental movement persuade political action? We've tried vinegar, who is working on operation honey? Surely the best argument is to appeal to people's wallets. Is anyone trying other methods of persuasion? If so, why don't we hear about it?

The subject I want to read more about is leadership. I've never really seen myself as a leader but as my career progresses I'm thinking about it more. What is leadership and can you develop it or are you born with it?

What things are puzzling you right now?

Why some people are still homophobic?

Why are domestic flights and trains so expensive?

Why so many people, even feminists, get squeamish about women proposing?

Why are weddings so expensive (both hosting and attending)?

Why men don't want to look after their small children and why employers don't make an effort to support them to do this.

I'm puzzled right now by the fact that there seems to be so little on TV – and why is that always the case over the summer, despite there being so many channels and the fact I'm quite easy to please.

How do you recover from a mental health problem when NHS mental health services are so oversubscribed? Where you can find proper support and help?

Where can you buy decent clothes when you are over 40 without looking like the lovechild of Rihanna and Timmy Mallet?

Who buys Black Eyed Peas albums (and other stuff I consider rubbish)? Also, who shops at QVC and all those other shopping channels? I've never met anyone. Ever.

Women who wear high heels all the time, in any circumstances, such as when taking their kids to the farm (yes, really).

What possesses people to go out without a coat in winter, particularly for a night out?

People who only eat raw food. How do they not starve to death?

I can't say anything puzzles me. With the power of the internet I look up every puzzle straight away. Although, saying that, I was puzzled how the villain in *Frozen* seems to be taken with Anna when they first meet so why does he then double-cross her. I did google that (really) and no explanation was really offered, though some people suggested that the lyrics of 'Love is an Open Door' do give the game away.

I have been wondering about *Frozen* but, for me, I've been preoccupied with how everyone is continually gushing about how it's so great to have these female leads. I'm supposed to be so delighted that the sisters' relationship is central to the story but I was too distracted (read disappointed) that they still had impossibly tiny wasp waists and ginormous eyes (thyroid condition alert!). Why can't they look like normal people? In *Toy Story* the children looked normally proportioned. Why can't a princess story do that? Plus, I'm supposed to be grateful that they made Prince Charming a rake. Well, maybe I would if they didn't immediately replace him with some rugged entrepreneur guy. And sure it's sisterly love that saved the day, but I was too aggrieved by that point to congratulate the film-makers for their liberal-mindedness. End result: I'm fuming and more cross at this 'progressive' film than I am generally. Maybe because it's the same old garbage masquerading as feminism.

Have you noticed any new trends recently?

Male feminists.

Jumpsuits (I found one I love and now approve of them).

Shirts buttoned up to the neck. (Again, I approve. Basically, my signature look with a jumper from October to March.)

This is not new, but it never seems to stop increasing – articles about mindfulness; articles about non-proven or disproven 'alternative' treatments. I am fascinated by the gullibility in relation to quackery.

Crazy eyebrows that look like they've been tattooed on. (Not that new, but you see it a lot these days.)

Fried capers. Now I love a caper with smoked salmon, in Caesar salad dressing, as a nice addition to olive tapenade, even those giant caper berries with charcuterie, but lately there has been fried capers with everything. Enough! Remember that scene in *The Devil Wears Prada* where Meryl Streep's character explains how Anne Hathaway's character comes to be wearing a particular shade of blue? I'd like the same thing, but for fried capers. Food trends drive me a bit bonkers – they are a nice change at first, but then menus are saturated with the same three ingredients. It's like junior high fashion, but for food.

My story – Laura Ferreiro

Laura Ferreiro is a freelance writer and former West Coast Editor of *NME*.

I noticed during my day-to-day routine of reading music publications and the press releases in my inbox that several indie or alternative musicians' names had been coming up in relation to films. It was the French indie band M83 scoring the sci-fi film *Oblivion* that initially caught my attention, as well as Jonny Greenwood of Radiohead who had written the memorable and controversial score to the Daniel Day Lewis film *There Will Be Blood* and the film version of the Lionel Shriver's *We Need To Talk About Kevin*.

It occurred to me that these young(ish), hip musicians seemed to be getting some plum film assignments instead of the old guard of film composers, such as Howard Shore and Hans Zimmer.

I had also just interviewed the director of *Tron: Legacy* and we had talked about indie French electronic duo Daft Punk's pivotal role in creating the music for his film. So it occurred to me there might be a trend there. I had also read in some interviews with indie bands that had worked on films, that the films' directors had often grown up listening to these indie artists, many of whom were around the same age.

I asked some publicist contacts whether they knew of any other indie artists who were trying their hand at scoring films, and they provided a few good leads. Since this was about the business side of things and had to do with both music and film, I thought it would be a perfect fit for *Variety*'s quarterly 'Music for Screens' issue.

My editor liked the idea and I ended up interviewing several notable indie musicians who explained why they thought this was a trend, what had attracted them to scoring films, and how writing for films presented unique and welcome challenges that took them outside of their comfort zone.

I also asked a few friends who work in various professions the following:

1   Can you tell me something interesting about your work – either something that has happened or something you enjoy doing or something interesting you have found out recently.
2   Can you tell me something bad about your work – either something irritating or someone annoying or the thing you enjoy least.

And I got the following answers:

Something interesting about my work – there has recently been a change in the law that means that all big companies have to put their audit contract out for tender every ten years. This has had a massive impact on the way we work – people that would previously have been working on audits are now spending all their time pitching for new ones, and companies that haven't changed auditor for 50 years are now having to go out to tender. The intention was that more small firms would get big audit contracts; in practice all that happens is that the big four firms swap the contracts around between us.

What I really enjoy is variety, but within a unifying theme, i.e. I'm interested in health issues, but couldn't bear to work on the same issue over and over again, as academics do.

I like seeing projects through from an initial idea and bid to a finished report and having personal responsibility for their success.

A thing that has happened is that I recently launched an intranet site which essentially covers career development. I loved doing it as it was a real challenge and was going nowhere but I turned the project round and have had loads of great feedback on the site.

I recently interviewed one of the most impressive candidates I have met in a long while. She is about my age, and clearly very good at what she does. But the most interesting thing I found was that she came back earlier than planned from maternity leave (after twelve weeks) and has a very different view on being a mummy to me – and she doesn't have a stay-at-home partner.

The thing that annoys me is the level of bureaucracy involved with getting a meeting room booked, even with two months' notice.

Too many meetings about nothing. These days I always ask: What's it about? Who's going to be there? What papers will we have in advance? How long will it last?

Recycling of old ideas with new jargon as though they are new. This is a hazard of being an older worker. It is necessary to bite back the urge to say 'Yeah, we did that...'.

What I don't enjoy is manual data collection and manipulation which I was doing some of earlier this year. Mind numbing.

Unfortunately for the external recruiter these days, companies are (understandably) trying to do more recruitment directly through their internal recruiters to save costs, which means my job is harder and I am increasingly told off by people who hold quite a bit of power and can be quite snooty about it. And then I have to remind myself that there are really much bigger things in life than recruitment spats in the workplace! My children, in particular, have given me a better perspective on that.

What a mine of ideas all of the above are. Here are just a few of them with some of the ideas they sparked:

'The subject I want to read more about is leadership. I've never really seen myself as a leader but as my career progresses I'm thinking about it more. What is leadership and can you develop it or are you born with it?'

- How to develop leadership skills – at home, in the workplace, with friends.
- How to be led – even if you are a leader sometimes you need to let other people take charge. Here's how to let yourself be led.
- Leadership lessons to use at home – what leadership skills from the workplace can help your home run more smoothly.
- How to help your children develop leadership skills.

'Crazy eyebrows that look like they've been tattooed on. (Not that new, but you see it a lot these days.)'

- Beauty treatments that people regret – interesting to look at people who had things done 20 or 30 years ago or longer to see how they feel about it now.
- Who are the people who invent new beauty treatments?
- Beauty secrets from around the world – what do people do in other countries that we might like to know about ourselves? Related to this – what do people consider beautiful around the world that maybe we don't.
- I have never... shaped my eyebrows, worn make-up, shaved my legs, etc. Talk to people who have never ever tried popular beauty treatment about this choice.

'Too many meetings about nothing. These days I always ask: What's it about? Who's going to be there? What papers will we have in advance? How long will it last?'

- Do you really need that meeting? Articles for a range of business-related publications on how to ensure that a meeting is necessary.
- Alternatives to meetings – quick phone calls, email round robins, etc.
- Tips for meetings – how to act to ensure you don't get saddled with too many tasks in a meeting.
- Doodling is obvious, but what other things can you do to keep yourself entertained in a boring meeting?
- How to chair an effective meeting.

Task: Questions for friends

Come up with a list of questions you could ask your friends that might lead to some interesting ideas. I have given you ten to get you started. See if you can come up with ten more.

(Continued)

(Continued)

1 What was the best and worst thing about your last holiday?
2 If you could only eat one type of international cuisine ever again, what would it be?
3 In an ideal world, how many children would you like and why?
4 What's your best Christmas (or other festival) memory from childhood?
5 Recommend me a book to read – why do you recommend it?
6 What do you wish you had done differently at your wedding?
7 Do you have advice for your teenage self?
8 What is your current favourite item of clothing and why?
9 What's on your current to-do list?
10 What are you doing next weekend?
11 _____
12 _____
13 _____
14 _____
15 _____
16 _____
17 _____
18 _____
19 _____
20 _____

A friend of mine once came back from a party horrified that she had taken an instant dislike to someone she had just been introduced to. It had never happened to her before and she was shocked. It happened to me, I told her, all the time. (She is clearly a much nicer person than me!) I wouldn't write about my friend and her experiences specifically, but I would use the conversation to write a piece on why we shouldn't judge people immediately, or whether to trust our instincts on this kind of thing, or how to act in different situations to make the best possible impression, etc.

In fact, everything that ever happens to you or anyone you know is a feature idea. Why did you order the drink you did? How often do you eat out and has this changed from the previous generation? Who taught you to boil an egg? Could we live without toilet paper? Is turning 40 the new 30? What hairstyles work best for which jobs? What should you do if you cut yourself and other essential first aid? How often should you change your toothbrush? Is there such a thing as friendship for life or do friendships ebb and flow? How can you wean yourself off your iPhone? Do correspondence courses work? Etc.

Task: The nicest person you know

Think of the nicest person you know. Ask yourself what makes them nice. Did they do something particularly kind for you or are they just generally an all-round nice person? Work out why you like them (perhaps they made you a cake) and come up with some feature ideas based on this (ten kind things you could do to make your neighbour's day).

Do the same for the least nice person you know.

My story – Ellie Levenson

Ellie Levenson is the author of this book and a freelance journalist. She lectures in journalism at Goldsmiths College, University of London.

Sometimes you play around with an idea and it's only when a suitable phrase or acronym occurs to you that you start to see how the article might work and how you can pitch it to an editor.

Several years ago I had a short-lived job that I really hated. It was only after starting the job that I heard stories from other people who had worked there about how awful it was for them too. The same thing happened to a close friend of mine who had a job that didn't work out, and who only found out after he arrived that his team had received training before he arrived, for being dysfunctional. I started to think that perhaps employers should be forced to disclose this kind of information before people accepted jobs – information such as staff retention rates, how many people get internal promotions, how quickly people move up the pay scale, etc.

This was shortly after Home Information Packs (HIPs) had been introduced for people selling their house and I realised that this acronym could be adapted for my idea – so I came up with Job Information Packs (JIPs). It meant I could pitch the idea with terms of reference that could be easily understood, as in 'you've heard of HIPs, now how about JIPs?'

The piece appeared as a cover story for the 'Work' section of the *Guardian*, which no longer exists, as quite a conventional multi-source feature – I spoke to people who had had bad experiences with jobs, and people who worked in human resources and for trade unions. I also spoke to politicians and lawyers. It was set up as an article posing it as a suggestion and asking readers whether they thought it was a good idea and inviting them to contribute to the debate online.

5 Getting ideas from the news

One of the greatest sources of feature ideas is the news. Huge numbers of features are written in response to news stories, from pieces that appear very quickly, to in-depth analysis of the stories behind the news, to features only connected to the original story by a fine thread, where a news story has inspired a feature writer to go off in a completely different direction.

If you are a feature writer working in-house then the news will probably be the main source of the stories you write, be it a daily newspaper with very short turnaround features or a monthly glossy consumer magazine where your features may respond to news of a new fashion collection or a statistic that appears in a news story about the average age of divorce or the cost of gym membership.

But if you are a freelance feature writer needing ideas that are unlikely to be generated in-house, you have to think about the news differently, looking for angles that can't be covered by journalists working in-house to tight deadlines, and that will still be relevant for a future publication date.

It is important to remember that even when using previously published articles for inspiration for your own idea, you should remain questioning and search for your own story. Take a news story that appeared on the BBC website while I was writing this book:

> More than one in ten three-year-olds have tooth decay, the first survey of the age group shows. Public Health England researchers checked the teeth of nearly 54,000 children … They found 12 per cent of children had evidence of tooth decay … Large variations were found from place to place in the study.

Taken at face value this leads to ideas including:

- What happens when your young child needs dental work? How to help them through this.
- How to persuade children to have their teeth brushed – what tricks and techniques have other parents used that have worked?

- How does the Department of Health intend to tackle this problem?
- Which areas are worst and why (and which are best and why)?
- Is this just sugary drinks or are more healthy culprits (e.g. raisins and dried apricots) involved? A look at what you should and shouldn't give your children from this perspective.

But you shouldn't just take the article at face value. Although the piece says this is the first survey of its kind, you might like to talk to dentists to see whether they think this is a problem that is getting better or worse. If better, perhaps you could write a piece on why this is getting better and the great public health success that is children's dental health. It is easy to assume from the news article that the situation is getting worse and unless you delve into this more deeply you won't know, and could miss a good feature idea.

Tip: Think about the less obvious

You may have a chart showing house prices in the UK this year and your initial thought might be concerning the incredibly expensive ones or the cheapest ones. But don't forget to wonder what an average house looks like and who lives in it. See if you can visit a few average houses, or follow the story of some people as they try to sell or buy a house.

One of the first things that someone learning to write news is told is to make sure you answer the questions who, what, where, why and when, and sometimes how, in the first sentence, or at least in the first two sentences. Although writing features is a completely different skill to writing news, it is handy to hold onto those six questions when it comes to getting ideas from the news, and use them to probe deeper into the story.

For example, you might apply these to a story about an armed robbery at a local supermarket and come up with the following:

- Who – Why target a supermarket? (The supermarket is the 'who' in this case.) Is this a new type of crime? Are banks too difficult as a target these days?
- What – No ideas.
- Where – Where are the crime hotspots in the country? Why?
- Why – In the age of CCTV and DNA testing, what makes people think they'll get away with it?
- When – Is there a time of day or day of the week or time of year, etc. when most armed robberies take place? Why is this?
- How – How did they get hold of the weapon? A feature looking at the route weapons take into the country and how people buy them.

Or, to take another idea, a news story about a celebrity launching a range of underwear at a high street store:

- Who – There are lots of beautiful and sexy celebrities but what makes a celebrity the right one to launch an underwear range?
- What – How much do celebrities get involved in the design of products that bear their name?
- Where – How do you match the celebrity to the shop?
- Why – How much money can such an endorsement earn for a shop? Or earn for a celebrity? Why do people like to buy things branded in such a way?
- When – No ideas.
- How – What are the stages of a celebrity endorsed range, from the initial approach to the products being in the shop?

Task: Stories from today's news

Take any story from today's news. Make a list of the who, what, where, why, when and how in the news story. Then use these as inspiration for features.

Example:

Describe the news story: Shadow Attorney General resigns her role after tweeting a 'judgemental' picture of England flags on a house on by-election day in the Rochester and Strood constituency.

	Use the news story to answer the questions	What features ideas are inspired by this?
Who	Shadow Attorney General	None
What	Resigned after tweeting a picture of a house with England flags	Rules of tweeting – what you need to know about twitter and social media before you are let loose with your thoughts and opinions – can they be seen forever? What counts as offensive? Can anyone look up your comments, etc?
Where	Rochester and Strood (England)	What do these flags really mean to people living in this area (and others)? Are flags ever 'just flags'?
Why	The photograph was said to be judgemental and snobby	Being judged changed my life – a case study based feature on people who felt judged or laughed at and how this made them change their lives

| When | Last night/on by-election day | When all the focus is on a particular town (i.e. during a by-election campaign) what happens when the cameras have left? |
| How | Picture was on Twitter. Resigned after making her party's leader very angry and an outcry from voters | What is a resigning issue (in any job)? When is it best to resign and when is it best to be sacked? |

Your turn:

Describe the news story:		
	Use the news story to answer the questions	*What features ideas are inspired by this?*
Who		
What		
Where		
Why		
When		
How		

You should also think, every time you read or hear a news story:

- What isn't being reported?
- Why has this made the news now?

The answers to these two questions can lead to multiple feature ideas.

My story – Gary Younge

Gary Younge is a feature writer and columnist for the *Guardian*. He is based in the United States.

A good feature article either has to represent something very broad or very narrow. Either something very specific that you could not really imagine in any other place – some amazing one-off that in some way represents the singular, or be about something or someone indicative of something broader.

(Continued)

(Continued)

I generally go for things that are broader and seem some kind of trend or general phenomenon. Having written a lot about immigration, for example, I decided to drive the full distance of the American–Mexican border as a way of understanding and looking at this geographical fault line. That was a geographical route that led to a broader cultural and political issue. In that sense the border became a motif really.

I was trying to work out what would be a different way of looking at this subject and that might be more arresting than general scene-based articles that had been written. Quite often your ideas get into your head in an almost subconscious way. You read one story about the border somewhere and then you read something else about Latinos somewhere else and then after a while the critical mass of themes and images out there get into your brain and you think 'Oh, maybe I should do it this way'.

I can't remember exactly but I do know by the time I came to write that piece I had been down to border areas and felt the weirdness that you find there. One time I suddenly came across a border post in America and was asked for my passport and I didn't have it as I wasn't going abroad and that set me thinking. That was three years earlier. Quite often ideas can be very slow burners. Then a couple of years later there were big Latino pro immigration demonstrations, and looking back on it I think I must have been looking for a way to understand those, for myself as well as for my reader.

Some years ago I wrote an article about the treatment of Roma people across Europe. This was when they were expanding the EU. There had been referenda in various countries and I remember looking at a map in the paper and an article was detailing what different countries had to do in order to join. In Bulgaria, Slovakia and the Czech Republic, the treatment of the Roma was a significant issue. I thought it was intriguing, that the treatment of a group of people I had some knowledge of and considerable interest in might be some kind of obstacle to these countries joining. I then realised they are the largest ethnic minority group in Europe and thought 'When do we ever talk about them?'. And I mentioned it in conference one morning and the features editor said 'Why don't you do something about that?', so then I had to try to work out how. It's not that I'd never thought about the Roma before. I had and I'd done a couple of articles about them before, but this was one article in the paper that tried to bring together a kind of fuller notion of this being an interesting subject.

To some extent, as a journalist you are amassing information the whole time and connecting it to things that aren't immediately related but that still have a connection in your mind for whatever reason. I studied languages at university. I lived abroad. I am Black. I was interested in race relations. I had some knowledge of the EU. All of these things, from my readings of Malcolm X to my understanding of the EU to my interest in migration, none of which are necessarily immediately relevant or connected, came together in one thing. But, of course, you can't draw people into a story about Roma people by talking about the EU; you have to talk about the people who are affected and make them real in some way. The original thing that gets me interested isn't going to be the thing that draws readers into the piece. To that extent it's all storytelling.

I also think that good feature writing always has a strong news-led element. I remember doing a piece about all the children who were shot in one day, at the time eight children were shot dead every day in the United States. They said, pick a day, find the kids and report on them. That is an idea that came from a single, constant, statistic but never stops being newsy because child shootings are always happening.

One way feature writers turn news into features is to take a bigger story and give it a local angle. That is – thinking back to the ideas equation – change your audience. So, a feature looking at the background to the story about the kidnapping of Nigerian schoolgirls by terrorist group Boko Haram might be localised by talking to Nigerian people living in your community about their experiences, or a story about a hurricane in the Caribbean may lead to a feature in the UK looking at the impact on the price of exotic fruits, and finding alternatives from other parts of the world.

For example, a major natural disaster somewhere may have an impact on whether people can get to school. It may give rise to conditions that lead to poor public health. It may stop air travel to the region, and so on. And each of these situations leads to potential features. A few such feature ideas might be:

- A look at people whose education was curtailed in the past due to natural disasters. For example, an earthquake flattened their school 20 years ago and they never went back into education. What happened next to these people?
- Some people in temporary housing may have developed a new way to filter dirty water – you might want to look at this and other inventions that have come out of emergencies.
- Living conditions may have led to a return of unusual diseases – perhaps these warrant a feature, or a look at what the world is doing, or should be doing, to combat the spread of this disease
- What happens when there is no air travel to a country? Look at the people stranded abroad unable to get home. Where are they now? What are they doing? How are they getting money to live? Are their careers suffering?
- How do you build a temporary airport out of nothing? A look at the emergency teams who go to disaster-hit regions and do just this.

Don't forget that you can get many new feature ideas just by changing the subject, angle or audience (though I have specified no audience here). You might take the last idea on that list, for example, and change it to 'How do you build a temporary hospital out of nothing?', or 'How do you build a temporary school out of nothing?' or even 'How do you make a temporary shelter for a family?'.

Remember, to be news something new has to have actually happened. To be a feature, you just have to tell your reader something that is new to them.

These methods don't just apply to large-scale emergency situations, such as earthquakes, bombs, hurricanes, wars, etc. Nearly all ideas work on local levels as well as national, international and supranational levels.

Take, for example, a burst water main that is taking a long time to fix. This may make a small news story for a local newspaper or website. But as a feature writer you can then be inspired by that news story to think about the implications for lots of different people, groups and subjects in much the same way as the example above. So you might think about the burst water main in terms of its impact on public transport, local businesses or public health, for example. When I do that, some of the following ideas occur to me:

- How do public transport companies plan for such events and decide alternative routes? And how are these routes communicated to, and remembered by, the drivers?
- If routes are affected then what about people who live on the closed bit of route and rely on public transport? Is there a scheme in place to alert social services, for example, to older people who can no longer get a bus to the shops to get their food shopping or to the bank or post office to collect their pension?
- How do small business owners plan for unexpected forced closures or lack of footfall? Is there insurance for this? Perhaps a case study based piece for a publication aimed at shop owners looking at how small businesses have planned for such events or overcome them, with guides on how to do this.
- What to do if you see a burst water main (or other problem, such as a large pothole) as a member of the public. Who do you report this to? What should they do about it? What should you do if the problem persists?
- What to do if you have an accident as a result of the problem (e.g. slip over in a puddle of water caused by the leak). How to log the incident. When you are entitled to compensation, etc.
- How local schools plan for emergencies and closures? Where would be an alternative place for students to sit exams if the running of the school were disrupted?

Of course, things are happening that go unreported all of the time. Not every burst water main makes it into the local newspaper. Not every earthquake gets reported. There are wars in countries which many of us have never thought about and terrible things happening to groups we have never heard of. There are inventions that never get any column inches, great speeches that are never written down and miraculous recoveries from illness that no one beyond the patient's family ever knows about.

As a feature writer one of your jobs is to look not just at what has been reported and be inspired to write stories based on that, but also to think about what hasn't made the news and why. Sometimes the moment has passed to get coverage for something in the news pages, but you can explore it through a feature long after the event is actual news (i.e. something new has happened).

Much as in the earlier chapter on getting ideas from objects, it is a good idea to develop a list of people, groups or subjects that you think about in relation to news events to see whether it helps you to come up with an interesting angle for a feature.

For example, you might want to think about:

- the young
- the old
- employed people
- unemployed people
- students
- homeless people
- homeowners
- people who rent
- business owners
- public sector workers
- politicians
- trade
- public health
- travel
- teachers
- the military
- energy
- utilities, e.g. water and electricity
- sport
- schools
- hospitals
- shops
- pets
- wild animals.

Or you might find it easier to think about stories in relation to people you know. Take a news story about the Government cutting a particular benefit, for example. How does this affect:

- you
- your parents
- your siblings
- your grandparents
- your children
- your children's friends
- your friends
- your neighbours.

Maybe try thinking further afield, in terms of how it affects:

- the owner of my local corner shop
- the person who serves me at the supermarket
- the person I wave to when walking my dog
- the parents I chat to in the school playground
- the people who teach my children
- the person who cleans my office
- the carer who helps my elderly neighbour
- the porter at my local hospital.

And so on.

As you think about these ideas and develop your own way of working and your own specialisms you'll come up with your own list to set against each news event.

The above technique is particularly helpful because all features (and all news) need to relate to the reader in some way. This may be because the event has a direct impact on their lives, or because it is acting as a warning, or an opportunity, or to create empathy with another person or community, or to give you information, or as a call to action, but in some way it must relate to the reader or there is no point in publishing it.

You may also want to develop your own list of questions to ask about each news event that interests you. For example:

- Has this happened before? If so, what happened next?
- Is it likely to happen again?
- Whose fault is it?
- How can this be prevented/encouraged in future?
- What is the emotional impact of this on me?

At the time of writing this section there is a story on the front page of the BBC News website with the headline 'Danny Alexander to call for fuel price cut' and the first sentence is: 'The Chief Secretary to the Treasury is to urge petrol and diesel distributors to cut prices further after recent declines in the cost of oil.'

Of course, everyone's lives and circumstances are different so there is no point telling you the specific impact it has on your life, but think about this story in relation to people you know. First, there is a direct impact on people who buy fuel. But, taken further, there is an impact on anyone who uses a taxi or bus or aeroplane or other form of transport that uses fuel. Take it further again and there is an impact on anyone who ever uses anything that is moved around. So, unless you are entirely self-sufficient and never go anywhere other than by foot, bike or person-powered boat, then that is you and everyone you know, as the cost of fuel has an impact, for example, on the transportation of food to shops or delivery of goods we order online or transportation of cars from foreign factories to our country.

If you have a list of people you know, you can start thinking how it would affect them. Some examples are given below:

- If fuel prices do go down, what might you use the money you saved for? And what impact would that have. For example, would you use it to buy a bunch of flowers instead, in which case will lots of people do this and will your local florist notice a boom?
- How will schools use any money saved – do lower fuel prices mean more textbooks? What impact might this have on your child?
- What about the local hospital – how do public bodies, such as hospitals, budget for goods that have fluctuating prices? Is there a feature that could be written on how this is done or the person whose job it is to balance the books?
- If fuel prices go down will companies use more lorries – what impact might this have on your friend or neighbour who is a lorry driver? Will there be more work for them?

And so on.

Some other potential ideas to explore could be:

- People in rural communities who are having difficulty buying what they need because shops are limiting their trips to wholesalers due to fuel costs.
- Services that may become unaffordable if fuel prices continue to rise and the impact this might have (e.g. school buses, meals on wheels, dial-a-ride).
- People who need a car to get around for whatever reason who are limiting their trips due to fuel costs.
- Trends noticed by people who work in petrol stations (e.g. people buying smaller amounts of fuel, more people stealing fuel).
- Recession crimes – when prices are high and incomes low, what crimes increase (e.g. stealing fuel from the petrol tanks of cars).
- People who use alternative forms of fuel (both legally and illegally).

My Story – Patrick Wrigley

Patrick Wrigley is a freelance journalist based in Turkey.

I wrote a long form feature for the US website *Roads and Kingdoms* (www.roadsandkingdoms.com) about my search for a British man, Donald Mackenzie, who went missing on Mount Ararat looking for Noah's Ark. He was climbing to look for a 'find' announced by a Hong Kong group, which later turned out to be an elaborate fraud.

I'd been meaning to climb Ararat for years so the mountain was in the back of my mind. Then I was putting together weekly reading lists of interesting articles on Turkey and the Middle East for my blog and decided to do a search about Mount Ararat. I found a news piece about Donald's disappearance and thought the story seemed to have everything – mystery, an ancient relic, fraud. I was desperate to find out more.

I went for a longer form article (the initial draft was 3,000 words) partly because that's the form of journalism I'm most interested in and want to develop and partly because the story has a lot of elements (the disappearance, the hoax, the context of the tourism industry in Eastern Turkey) so I felt it needed space. Also, the short form news piece had already been done at the time of his disappearance.

How I approached it was determined by what was possible to report on my budget. The most straightforward way to do this was as a travel piece, so my audience had to be people interested in adventure travel. But also, given the situation in Eastern Turkey, people interested in politics as well. And there is an element of a boy's own adventure, so I was thinking of the men's magazine audience initially.

I had a limited budget so wasn't able to hire fixers, translators or go to Hong Kong (where the Ark fraud originated). So it really became a story exclusively about my trip out East to climb Ararat and find out about Donald rather than what I had originally envisaged, which was an even longer piece with less of my voice in there. I had also planned to include sections on the history of ark searching and the development of the modern industry but, given the limited information I had for the dramatic elements of the story, I thought this additional context would dilute the story's power. I was lucky, however, to find and climb with Donald's former guide who told me about finding his tent on the mountain and provided me with lots of information and colour.

If you specialise in writing about a specific topic, you will be able to come up with a specialised list of people or businesses to think through for each news item. If you write about personal finance for example, your list might include:

- people with mortgages
- renters
- landlords

- people in debt
- payday loan users
- lenders
- banks
- building societies
- credit unions
- employers
- employees
- unwaged.

If you specialise in writing about crime you might apply each piece of news to:

- lawyers
- judges
- criminals
- victims
- police officers
- probation officers
- members of the prison service.

These are crude lists to illustrate the point, but as you get to know your areas you will work out your own lists to apply each news story to in order to see where the features may lie.

Another way to do this is to make a list of the kinds of people who read the publication you are targeting and then set that list against all the news stories you are looking at.

For example, you may want to write for a particular glossy consumer magazine aimed at professional women in their thirties and forties. As you read through the news you can think about how each story may affect them. And the good news here is that you have an automatic hook for your pitch as well.

Here's an example:

Professional women in their thirties and forties

News story (headlines from BBC News website)	Ideas for this audience
A prototype inflatable incubator for prematurely born babies has been picked as the 2014 winner of the James Dyson Award for engineering	What to do if you have a great idea for an invention Women in their thirties and forties who invented things

(Continued)

(Continued)

Professional women in their thirties and forties	
Canadian astronaut Commander Chris Hadfield's cover of David Bowie's track *Space Oddity*, recorded on board the International Space Station, is back on YouTube	Do you waste too much time on YouTube?
	Why messing around on the internet is good for you – how to use what you find to inspire you
	Why messing around on the internet is bad for you – how to avoid the temptation
	Women who have made careers from 'messing around on the internet'
A portrait of a Parisian actress by Edouard Manet has set a new auction record for the French impressionist	Why you should be investing your spare cash in art
	How to invest your spare cash in art
	How to buy at an auction
	I've always wanted to be an artist's model – experiential piece
	A picture of me sold for millions – talk to women who were in photographs or paintings that have sold for lots of money
Dairy Crest, maker of Cathedral City cheese and Country Life butter, announces a big slump in profits and the sale of its dairies business	Could you cope without cheese?
	How I learned to love cheese – take someone who doesn't like cheese and teach them to like it, starting with mild cheeses working up to stinky cheeses
	How to make your own cheese at home
Happiness nose dives as you hit middle age – but only if you live in affluent Western countries, latest research suggests	Are you prepared for your 'happiness dip'?

And don't forget that feature formula – Idea = subject + angle + audience (+ hook)

Ideas from news – Becky Gardiner

Becky Gardiner has been a commissioning editor for various magazines, newspapers and websites. She lectures in journalism at Goldsmiths College, University of London.

Working on a features desk of a daily news publication, you start with the day's news. First, you consider the day's big stories: you look at the different ways the story has been covered in various publications, and think about what's been left out and what hasn't been discussed yet. These gaps in the story can be fertile ground for features. It might be that the story is only being discussed from one perspective, for example, and by switching focus you can get a new angle. So, if everyone's talking about Eastern European immigration in terms of the problems it creates for UK nationals, you might think of sending someone to a town in Eastern Europe which is suffering a 'brain drain' to Britain and talk to people there, or you might find a British town where migrants have been welcomed with open arms for some reason. Or, if the story has so far been covered in a very newsy, fact-based way, it might be enough to simply talk to lots of ordinary people who are part of the story – migrants and UK nationals – in the towns where they are concentrated. These news-based features can be very fast or much slower, depending on how long you feel the story will remain newsworthy.

You are also looking to tell the stories of people who embody or personify the story. For example, if some new fact about older mothers is reported, you might try to find someone who is an older mother who can talk about her own experience. You need to think about what – or who – is being left out in the telling of the story.

You also want to think about the history behind a news event. For example, when everyone was talking about the television programme *Benefits Street* – a documentary series about a street in Birmingham which was billed as being Britain's most benefit-dependent street – the *Guardian*'s Jon Henley spent time in Birmingham archives to look at the history of the street. What he discovered changed the terms of the debate. Similarly, you might also want to throw things forward and look at the future – to take the older mothers example again, you might also want to think about what will happen if the trend continues, and mothers get older still.

Another good source of ideas is to take a local story and make it bigger, or take a big story and make it smaller. For example, if there is a news story about an initiative in British schools, you might look at how it compares to what other countries do to address the same problem. Or, if there is a story about the growing wealth gap internationally, you might look at the lives of two individuals – one from the poorest one per cent, one from the richest one per cent.

Ideas for quick reactive pieces can come from things people have said, too. While news is busy focusing on the thing itself, and people's responses to it, a feature writer can use it as a peg for a different kind of piece. An example that springs to mind is when some politician – I forget who – was asked the price of a loaf of bread, and didn't know the answer. Much was made of this: how out of touch politicians were, how rich they all were, etc. But we talked to journalist Felicity Lawrence, who has real expertise about pricing and food, and she wrote a great piece about how there is actually no such thing as the price of a loaf of bread – it can be sold for a few pence as a loss leader in a budget supermarket or for a fiver in an artisan bakery. This became a really interesting feature about how supermarkets manipulate both prices and the quality of what we eat.

Idea	Change subject	Change audience
What to do if you have a great idea for an invention	What to do if you have a great idea for a TV programme	
Women in their thirties and forties who invented things		Men in their thirties and forties who invented things
		Women in their seventies and eighties who invented things
Do you waste too much time on YouTube?	Do you waste too much time window shopping?	
Why messing around on the internet is good for you – how to use what you find to inspire you	Why window shopping is good for you – how to use what you see to inspire you	
Women who have made careers from 'messing around on the internet'	Women who have made careers from window shopping	Men who have made careers from 'messing around on the internet'
		Older people who have made careers from 'messing around on the internet'
Why you should be investing your spare cash in art	Why you should be investing your spare cash in wine	
How to invest your spare cash in art	How to invest your spare cash in wine	
How to buy at an auction	How to sell at an auction	
	How to buy direct from the artist	
I've always wanted to be an artist's model – experiential piece	I've always wanted to be an auctioneer – experiential piece	

A picture of me sold for millions – talk to men who were in photographs or paintings that have sold for lots of money

I was in a picture that became famous

No one knows that nude is me – an artist's model reveals all to their nearest and dearest

That's my mum – talk to people whose parents were in photographs or paintings that have sold for lots of money or become famous

Could you cope without wine?

Could you cope without coffee?

Could you cope without make-up?

Could you cope without your phone?

How I learned to love coffee – take someone who doesn't like coffee and teach them to like it, starting with latte working up to espresso

How to make your own yoghurt at home

Are you prepared for your hair to turn grey?

Are you prepared for your health to nosedive?

A picture of me sold for millions – talk to women who were in photographs or paintings that have sold for lots of money

Could you cope without cheese?

How I learned to love cheese – take someone who doesn't like cheese and teach them to like it, starting with mild cheeses working up to stinky cheeses

How to make your own cheese at home

Are you prepared for your 'happiness dip'?

My Story – Johanna Bell

Johanna Bell is a freelance journalist.

Just over a year ago I received a press release announcing that Fear of Missing Out (FOMO) costs the average Brit £1,463 a year. It also produced stats to say one in six Brits can't say no to social events even when they can't afford them, and that one in five feel depressed after seeing pictures online of activities they've missed.

I'd certainly noticed the term FOMO being mentioned on social media – it was a regular hashtag used in my Twitter feed and a few of my friends on Facebook would use it after posting up photos of a last-minute night out. I had one particular friend who went out every night without fail despite constantly vowing to stay in and save some money and catch up on sleep. She just couldn't say no. It seemed like a genuine growing trend and I thought it would make a good piece for the 'Sun Woman' section of the *Sun*, as they regularly explore new trends and phrases.

I pitched the idea of getting together a line-up of women who all suffer from FOMO to talk about it to my contact at 'Sun Woman', who had also seen the press release and had a similar idea. She commissioned me to find three women for the piece.

It was probably the easiest case study search I'd ever done – as soon as I posted it on Twitter I was inundated with women in their twenties who were all burned out and skint but still constantly going out. I took the three strongest case studies and cleared them with the editor. I got the women to keep a tally of how much they spent and what they spent it on over the next month, so we could do box-outs with the feature. There was one girl who spent £2,800 in one month and admitted she almost always feels run down and tired. Another earned a lot less than her friends, so stuck to soft drinks on most nights out so she could keep up with their social lives without bankrupting herself. The biggest thing for all of them was the fact that if they ever missed a night out or get together it would simultaneously be rubbed in their faces, as photos were uploaded on Facebook as soon as they were taken. That made me understand why it was a relatively new term being used.

The feature went down well with the editor and we ended up doing a follow-up just before Christmas, focused on women with FOMO over the busy Christmas party season. Their resounding message was: 'We'll sleep in January!'

Tip: Acronyms

If you can come up with a catchy acronym or new word to describe a trend or phenomenon, then that in itself can be a great feature idea. Think WAG (Wives and Girlfriends of male sports stars), staycation (having a holiday close to home), bromance (an intense male friendship) and frenemy (a friend who is really your enemy) to name a few.

6 Getting ideas from other (non-news) articles, including books, leaflets, the internet and any other printed matter

Everything you read should lead to dozens of ideas for other articles. The original article does not have to be a feature article, though it might be.

A news report on a local burglar receiving community service might lead to a feature on whether community service works or what community service actually is or a look at places in your community that have been improved by community service or a feature on different types of punishment or an analysis of why people become burglars or how to protect your own property or how you would react if your own child was a burglar or interesting burglars in literature or where the word swag comes from, and so on.

A theatre review on a new mime show might make you think about the origins of mime or great mime artists or perhaps it might make you consider an experiential piece on spending a day (or a week or a month or a year) not talking.

A controversial opinion piece suggesting we go to war in a particular country might make you want to write a feature looking at current wars going on that few of us know about, or how weapons have changed over the years, or what kind of person joins the military, or the most effective ways to campaign against war, or living war criminals yet to be brought to justice, or how does a country go from the Prime Minister deciding to go to war to soldiers actually being deployed and fighting.

An obituary might generate several ideas linked directly to the person who died or sparked from a single line about them. If the person has been married five times, for example, there are many ideas you may think of connected with this. If they enjoyed keeping chickens in their back garden, this may also lead to lots of ideas.

A feature on people who swim outside in cold weather may make you want to write a feature on the ten best places to swim outside. Or they might inspire completely different ideas, such as how do scientists work out when high tide will be?

Good ideas people are always reading. It doesn't have to be around a particular area of interest – ideas people read newspapers they pick up on the bus, leaflets in doctors' waiting rooms, billboards as they walk along the street. They don't sit twiddling their thumbs while their friends go to the toilet when they meet for coffee, but read the menu instead. It's like being a fidget, just with your mind rather than your body. As a consequence nothing that you read is a waste.

I found a book the other day that I think I was given as a stocking filler for Christmas one year. I hadn't read it at the time but I kept it, knowing it might come in handy one day (no wonder so many journalists are also hoarders!). It's called *Fascinating Celebrity Facts* and is written by Hannah Warner, and is quite literally 200 pages of facts about celebrities.

If I turn randomly to a page (page 37 in this case) I get a list of facts about celebrity bodies, including that the actor Barbara Windsor has size one feet and the actor Daryl Hannah has size eleven feet, that Billy Connolly has pierced nipples and Sean Connery has two tattoos on his right arm. Also that actor Patrick Stewart, lost all his hair at the age of nineteen and actor Sadie Frost suffered a collapsed lung when she was four years old.

And without thinking too long about it, the following ideas have come to me from this:

- Where to buy shoes if you have very small feet.
- Where to buy shoes if you have very big feet.
- Ten great pairs of shoes for people with small feet.
- Ten great pairs of shoes for people with big feet.
- How did we end up with standardised foot measurements – what is the history? Who decided it? Expand to clothes measurements.
- What are the best countries to go to for outsized clothing – for example, which countries have good clothes for tall people, fat people, big feet, small feet etc., based on the typical shape of their population.
- Made to measure shoes – worth the investment?
- How well do you know the person sitting next to you – they might look conventional but do they have hidden piercings? Talk to people with pierced genitals or other body parts about their 'secret' – does it make them feel naughty? Would they mind colleagues knowing? Is it empowering? Embarrassing? Look at tattoos as well as piercings.
- The impact of health problems you had as a child once you become an adult – do kids who have had major operations think of this as part of their identity? Does it impact on how they live their lives? What about parents – does it change how you parent? How do you sit a child down and tell them that, as a baby, they were very ill?

You'll probably have different ideas, and even if you came up with the same idea, it would work differently for different publications depending on the approach we each took.

My story – Keiron Pim

Keiron Pim is a freelance journalist and former feature writer for the *Eastern Daily Press*.

Flicking through the events listings and entertainment guides for the weeks ahead is a reliable way of finding features, not only the obvious kind, such as preview interviews with musicians or comedians soon to perform in your patch, but more tangential ones too.

For one, you can start noticing trends. Is a particular kind of dance class or fitness session apparently growing more popular? Examples would include capoeira, say, or boxercise or Zumba. Ask the organisers if you can go along to one with a photographer and write a first-person piece about what it involves and how you got on.

Another way is to use a one-off event as a launch-pad into a broader story. This is what I did as a feature writer for the *Eastern Daily Press* when I saw that Norwich Arts Centre was hosting an evening billed as 'High Impact: Literature from the Low Countries'. The event struck me as a modern example of a long history of cultural connection between Norfolk and the Netherlands, one going back at least to the Middle Ages and full of interesting little stories.

I wrote a two-page spread exploring this and showing how, centuries ago, Norfolk had closer ties with the land across the North Sea than it did with relatively remote parts of England. In those times the county some-times described as 'not on the way to anywhere' was actually, by virtue of its long coastline, a gateway to the rest of the world. From King's Lynn to Great Yarmouth, Norfolk towns subsisted on the exchange of goods across the sea, and this economic relationship bred a fruitful interplay of cultures.

Dutch cartographers created some of the earliest maps of Norfolk, and it was a Dutch engineer, named Cornelius Vermuyden, who brought his nation's expertise to bear in draining the Fens, turning a watery wilderness into richly fertile farmland that catalysed the East of England's agricultural industry.

Norwich's tradition of accepting refugees led to a moment in the late sixteenth century when one-third of the city's population were Flemish and Walloon Protestants who had fled persecution in their homelands. The 'Strangers', as they became known, introduced new ways of weaving and their custom of keeping canaries created a tradition reflected in Norwich City FC's nickname.

To give another couple of examples, the only English people painted by Rembrandt were a Norwich-based Protestant pastor and his wife, and the Dutch Old Masters influenced the Norwich School artistic movement of the nineteenth century.

Alongside this I wrote a panel about the event at the arts centre in which I profiled the six visiting writers.

It may seem obvious, but another way to get feature ideas is to read features that have already been published. We have already looked at changing the subject, angle or audience to come up with a new hook. For example, that piece on ten best hats for the beach – what happens if you change hat for bag? What happens if you change beach for mountain? What happens if look at alternatives to hats – scarves perhaps? What is the latest hat technology? The cheapest hat? The most expensive hat? The most popular hat? Unisex hats? What would a look at all the hats you have ever owned look like? What would happen if you decided to wear a hat every day for a year? What is current hat etiquette regarding wearing hats indoors? Where should you buy your hat? Where do famous people buy their hats? And so on.

But reading published features can be helpful in other ways too. One freelance colleague of mine used to subscribe to a publication aimed at toy-makers and toy sellers so she could be ahead of the game (excuse the pun) when it came to spotting trends and knowing what would be available in shops in due course, plus it meant she had a great stash of hooks and dozens of ideas when it came to compiling gift guides.

When you develop a specialist area like this it is often called a beat (or patch). A beat is an area that a journalist on a publication works on, and becomes an expert in. They are the person who will write the stories about that subject or geographical area, and will develop a list of contacts and a bank of knowledge so that they are the publication's go-to person for information about it.

As a features writer you too can develop your own beat. Sometimes this happens by accident – you write a feature on a subject which leads to a connected idea and, before you know it, you are the person who is known for covering this subject and more work on this kind of thing comes your way. Soon broadcasters are coming to you for comment on the subject and very often you are then asked to write opinion about this subject as well as features. You may even find yourself hearing about new developments and writing, or tipping colleagues off, about news.

When choosing your own beat or beats – your own area in which to become an expert – you either want a big subject that not many people know about, or a very small area of a bigger subject. Some random examples:

- the politics and culture of Armenia
- scientific research into diabetes
- the legacies of past Olympic Games
- football in Wales
- volcanoes
- urban gardening
- sea kayaking
- gang culture in London
- feminism in the under 25s
- trends in handbag design
- university admissions.

My story – Olivia Solon

Olivia Solon is technology editor at the *Daily Mirror* website and former deputy editor of *Wired* magazine.

When an innocuous-looking leaflet came through the post from my GP talking about how 'better information means better care', I almost ignored it. But I picked it up one day while waiting for the kettle to boil and it seemed a bit suspect. It appeared to mark a major change to how our medical data is stored – the plan was (and still is) to take all of the health records currently stored with your GP and collate them in a central database. The aim, at least nominally, is to make the NHS better. But there are huge risks involved in bringing data together in this way, and I'd not heard anything about it.

Having already experienced a data breach at the hands of the NHS, I knew how upsetting it could be, so I started to dig into the issue. After speaking to a number of privacy campaigners, patients and GPs, it became extremely obvious that no one really understood exactly what was going to be done with our medical records. There was a lot of fear that the government was planning to sell off our medical records to the highest bidder – people were most worried about insurance companies getting hold of them. So I decided to write a definitive explainer, which turned into a series of articles.

For the *Wired* audience, the focus was on the data protection aspect – is it technically possible to share data without running the risk that patients could be re-identified? *Wired* is a huge supporter of using data cleverly to make government more efficient, but this seemed to be being done without sufficient thought and without informed patient consent.

For the piece, I navigated my way through the convoluted media department of the NHS and eventually got to speak with Tim Kelsey, the guy heading up the initiative. He couldn't answer many of my questions, so I had to speak to a couple of other people he worked with, as well as security specialists, campaigners and GPs. The more I dug, the more complex it seemed – there was a lot of misinformation out there, which privacy activists were jumping on but that wasn't actually true. Then there were other details that were seemingly being fudged by the NHS. Furthermore, people in the NHS seem to think that everyone else understands the jargon of the NHS. So. Many. Acronyms.

Eventually I got to a pretty definitive article on the subject matter that broke the issues down in ways that anyone could understand and that was reflected in the web traffic the story attracted – and continues to attract.

Task: Read leaflets

Next time you see an information leaflet – pick it up and read it. Question everything it says. Can you get any feature ideas from it?

Task: Look at old publications

Find an old publication. Take any news article. Look at what happened next? Look at whether the analysis was correct? Look at whether such a thing could happen now?

Also look at any current feature or news story. Think about what the impact of it will be next week, next month, next year and in the more distant future.

A huge source of feature ideas are online chatrooms and forums. My current personal favourite is *Mumsnet*, which charges journalists for starting a thread but this doesn't mean you can't take inspiration from threads that have already been published, or from threads you start in your non-professional capacity. My favourite example of this is an article written by someone else that I know that used 'a recent thread on breastfeeding on *Mumsnet*' as a hook not knowing it was me who started the thread, not as a journalist but as a mum with a breastfeeding question.

If I go online now while writing this and have a look at the 'active' threads (threads that have been most recently commented upon) one is called '90s London'. It drew my attention as I was a teenager in London in the 1990s. In the initial comment that started the thread the poster said she had recently been into the centre of London and was surprised by how much things had changed and that she was starting to feel nostalgic for the London of her youth. She then named some places she missed, including the Mechanical Toy Museum and Neal Street East shop, both in Covent Garden. Other people on the thread joined in with the London places they felt nostalgic about.

Straightaway, before even reading any of the messages in response, this led to ideas for me. The shop she mentions was somewhere my mum and I went every year for a special day out when I was a child, and one of the other places she mentioned later in her post was where I first got chatting to my husband. So I started to think about the following articles:

- An article aimed at parents about how to create special memories with your child.
- A guide to a day out for parents and children in London.
- Where to go in London to buy quirky gifts.

Other posters were mentioning particular greasy spoon cafes or coffee shops and markets, and this led to the following ideas:

- How to recreate the perfect greasy spoon breakfast at home?
- Where to find a greasy spoon in X city.

- The eating habits of greasy spoon owners (do they all secretly eat healthily while giving us fried breakfasts?).
- What is the greasy spoon equivalent around the world?
- Now the country is saturated with coffee shops what is the next trend? (Have noticed a lot of ice cream bars recently.)
- How do independent coffee shops and small chains differentiate themselves from big chains – examples of successful ones?
- Why do we like to think of places as not being as good as they used to be? What is the nature of nostalgia – is it a way of protecting ourselves from getting old, by convincing ourselves that things used to be better?
- How areas regenerate.
- People who like to keep places crap – those who campaign against improvements to areas.

I also like to read threads about subjects I don't know about, such as adoption or military families, to see what people in that situation are talking about and what ideas come from it. My children aren't at school yet but I have noticed that a frequent subject popping up on education and Christmas threads is from parents wanting inspiration for what to give teachers as a thank you gift at Christmas and the end of an academic year – this fascinates me as I don't remember giving any gifts at all, except perhaps the occasional box of chocolates to an exceptional teacher at the end of the year. So in terms of ideas it has made me think about:

- Should you be allowed to accept gifts from pupils and their families (for a publication aimed at teachers).
- Ways that poor students feel left out (e.g. not being able to afford to give teacher presents, or Christmas cards to other children, etc.).
- Ten best gifts for teachers (aimed at parents of school-age children).
- The best gift I ever got (teachers talking about best gifts, with an emphasis on handwritten notes, etc.).
- Should we show extra appreciation to people who are just doing their job (e.g. should we give gifts to teachers, tips to workmen, etc?).
- What do you do with fifteen 'Best teacher' mugs – a lighthearted look at people who have too many of the same gift.

As well as being a regular reader of specific sites, specialist forums should be a go-to place for ideas if you come up with an interesting hook but have no idea attached to it, or hear that a specialist publication is looking for an idea. For example, perhaps on a trip to a museum you notice that a particular canoe was invented 100 years ago. So you have your hook. Go to a canoeing forum and find out what canoes are popular at the moment and you have the beginnings of a feature on the changing face of canoe design.

Tip: Search, follow and listen

Laurie Penny, freelance journalist and columnist.

I count finding ideas as part of the job, so for features and columns what I generally do is take half a day or even a whole day and go to a café and go on the internet and take a massive pad of paper and spend some time Googling. A lot of the time I go on sites like Reddit and Metafilter, sites that bring together lots of different links, and follow any link I feel interested in and wonder what stories haven't been written as well as noting the ones that have.

The other way of finding ideas is just by going to places and listening to people talk; having long conversations with people you meet and their friends and asking them what they think is interesting. Part of it is about being quiet and listening to what people say. You normally find most people have particular obsessions and interests that they are happy to talk about. So, one of my top tips is to have opinionated friends who aren't journalists and another is to budget time for thinking of ideas because if all you are doing is writing then you have no time to be creative and think of ideas.

My story – Linda Geddes

Linda Geddes is a freelance journalist and former features editor of *New Scientist*.

I got sent a short summary describing a paper in the *Journal of Experimental Biology*, summarising some research measuring maximal performance in bullfrogs. That might not sound like the most compelling story in the world but there were several things that gave me a flutter of excitement. First of all it talked about a country fair in rural California where people had a frog jumping competition. It also made reference to professional frog jockeys and rental frogs. And I thought 'what the hell is a "rental frog" and a "frog jockey"?' and I had to find out. On YouTube I found some extremely entertaining videos of the frog jumping competition.

This led to me writing an article for *New Scientist* called 'Hop-a-long strategy', looking at the work of the author of the paper, Henry Astley. He had a very colourful background, describing himself as 'a critters kind of guy'. I interviewed the organisers of the annual frog jumping competition and delved into its historical background. As it turned out, the competition was inspired by one of Mark Twain's earliest short stories, *The Celebrated Jumping Frog of Calaveras County*. I also managed to find a professional frog jumping family to interview. Interviewing that family provided a huge amount of colour and I tried to stay true to the original language they used to convey their characters.

So, from a very dry scientific abstract I managed to produce a rich and colourful feature filled with human stories. I wrote it as if I'd been there and described the spectacle of watching the frog jumping competition and then I cut to the frog researcher in his lab on the other side of the country, trying to find a solution to the same problem – how do you incentivize a frog to jump, and explored his background and why he was investigating this. The reason he was investigating this was to understand the limitations of muscle, which has implications for human physiology as well as understanding more about frogs. And then I described how the researcher went out to California to learn more about the techniques that professional frog jockeys use and how he's applied them in his own work.

New forms of social media develop all the time so it is hard to know what platform people will be using by the time you read this book. At the moment, Twitter is a big source of stories for journalists. You can either follow interesting people or organisations to see what they are thinking about and linking to, keep an eye on what is 'trending' (i.e. what is popular at any given moment) or search by specific words.

For example, if I type 'new campaign' into the search box on Twitter, my results include the following interesting tweets:

- A tweet from the *Sun* newspaper about how West Ham United Football Club is backing their awareness campaign for men to check their testicles for signs of testicular cancer. It comes with the hashtag #FeelEmFriday.
- The Royal Society for the Prevention of Accidents (RoSPA) tweeting about its new drink drive campaign.
- The United Nations tweeting about a UNHCR campaign to end statelessness.
- *Stylist* magazine tweeting about Romeo Beckham starring in a new advertising campaign for the brand Burberry.

If I search for 'must stop' my results include the following interesting tweets:

- An organisation called the Blue Planet Society calling on the BBC to 'stop shying away from big wildlife conservation issues' with a link to an article in the *Telegraph* that quotes wildlife cameraman Doug Allan saying that the BBC should capitalise on their wildlife programming by finding ways for viewers to make a difference.
- A Kenyan tweeter who says that to stop cattle rustling alternatives must be found.
- An Australian Green Party politician, Janet Rice, highlighting that Australia is the largest beneficiary of illegal logging in Papua New Guinea.

If I search for 'This is amazing' my results include the following interesting tweets:

- A Twitter user linking to a 3D paper artwork depicting an underwater city (which is indeed amazing).
- A car dealership in Northumberland tweeting about another car dealership in Portsmouth, congratulating them for making the 'Top 100 Most Influential Dealers on Twitter' list in *Car Dealer Magazine*.

All of these lead to multiple feature ideas with hooks. What's more, Twitter is so active (5,700 tweets per second and 500 million tweets per day in 2013, according to Twitter) that every time you do a search your results will be different and, of course, there are huge numbers of search terms that you can use that might bear fruit.

My story – Rebecca Lefort

Rebecca Lefort is a former journalist on the *Sunday Telegraph*.

When I was on the *Sunday Telegraph* I got loads of stories from following celebrities on Twitter. I created a list of audience-specific celebrities that our readers would be interested in. I wasn't necessarily looking for stories that the celebrity was trying to put out as that would get picked up by everyone and I wanted stories that would still be fresh by Sunday, so what worked for me were tweets that gave me an angle and a way in but not the whole story.

For example, I saw that Stephen Fry had tweeted a couple of pictures that looked like they were of the Harry Potter set so I screengrabbed them straight away. Within ten minutes he'd deleted them and tweeted that he'd been sent to the naughty step. We then did a big story – 'Harry Potter and the Mystery of the Vanishing Tweet'. It was picture-led and the kind of quirky thing that does really well.

Another was when Kirstie Allsopp got into an argument with Belinda Phipps, who was Chief Executive of the parenting charity NCT, about women's guilt over having Caesareans. Because they had a conversation that was quite antagonistic, that was enough of a hook to make a story about these two people having a fight. I was able to interview both of them for it and the fact that they had done it online was the hook.

For another story, the magician Paul Daniels tweeted a link to a sale of some of his props on eBay so I found someone to say that this could go against the Magic Circle promise not to disclose secrets, and I got nice pictures of his tricks and information about how they work.

There had been a news story in the daily papers about a new naked picture of Elizabeth Taylor and I was following Hugh Heffner on Twitter and he said that the picture was a fake and linked to a blog that claimed this. I followed it up and that became an article which also meant we could rerun the picture we were calling a fake, which was good visually. Hugh Heffner wasn't mentioned in the piece at all – that's just how I got the story.

Blogs are also a brilliant source of article ideas. I really like maps and was reading blogs about maps, partly to find stories and partly because I like reading them anyway. I found a story someone had written about a town called Argleton, in Lancashire. This town didn't exist but was on Google Maps, and because of the way that Google works it had its own life – you could search for jobs and schools in Argleton. But actually it was a phantom town. Google wouldn't confirm this but in the olden days when people made maps they would make deliberate mistakes to stop them being copied, and experts told me that's what they thought Google had done too. The blog post it came from wasn't even recent but because it hadn't been in the newspapers before we ran it, giving the blogger credit.

And another source of stories I used regularly were Parliamentary Questions. Members of Parliament can send a written question to any Government Minister and they are all published, with answers, on the parliamentary website. Sometimes the questions are constituency matters and sometimes national matters, and can be a huge range from incredibly boring to very quirky. What often comes out as a response is a statistic and statistics are fabulous and can be great news hooks. For example, someone asked how much Ministry of Defence civil servants had been paid in bonuses and the answer included a chart that showed results for the last six years. So obviously that could be used as the basis for many articles.

Sir Bob Russell is the Member of Parliament for Colchester. He likes animals a lot and he asked a Parliamentary Question about a dog called Darcy from the Urban Search and Rescue Unit who had gone with a team of Essex firefighters to help uncover people in rubble after an earthquake in Indonesia, as had lots of other search and rescue dogs from around Europe. But because of our quarantine laws he was stuck in a kennel on his return while the other hero dogs were wild and free. Bob asked whether anything could be done to help Darcy and the answer was no. So we did a story about 'poor Darcy'.

Another politician asked a question about a scheme in Portsmouth where they had been trialling a transport policy, and they asked whether it had brought down the number of accidents, and the answer revealed it hadn't, which was a great story along the lines of 'have the speed Nazis gone too far?'.

My story – Archie Bland

Archie Bland is Saturday features editor at the *Guardian*.

Some ideas you find in the penultimate paragraph of a local newspaper court report; some are thrust upon you by editors and PRs; some are the fruition of conversations with sources who have a story that has to be told. In my experience, though, the best are the ones that have bounced around your head for so long that you can't really remember where they came from. So it was with the piece of mine I've found most satisfying to write, about the former British tennis player, Jamie Baker.

Actually, I had the idea for a couple of years before I knew who Baker was.

This may sound weird; it certainly provides an object lesson in how no idea will survive contact with reality exactly as you conceived of it, and how closely you have to scrutinise your subject to make sure that your abstract pitch doesn't cloud a more interesting truth. Stories that go in surprising directions are bound to be livelier than the ones that wound up how you expected. They'll make you think harder, and make absolutely certain that the bigger story you're hoping to tell has some connection to reality. And if that means you have to start all over again, the results will be the better for it.

As a casual tennis fan, it's often struck me that there's no other sport where the superstars and the minnows compete in such close proximity, or with such regularity – and where the gap between the two is so slight and so vast at the same time. It's interesting that while the top ten earn millions, and the top 150 earn a living, the players just below that may be operating at a loss – even though their sport is a multi-billion pound industry. The 200th best footballer in the world might be in the premier league; the 200th best tennis player is deemed a loser, and participating in tournaments by paying hotel bills that frequently exceed the prize money on offer. Tim Henman was the fourth best tennis player in the world and the layperson tends to think of him as a loser. This is all nuts.

I remember when this vague idea crystallised into a determination to write about it: when James Ward, a surprising British winner in the first round of Wimbledon, said ruefully at his post-match press conference that the windfall made him wish he hadn't cancelled his Arsenal season tickets. I found that funny and sad and compelling, but I was in an editing job at the time. So I put it on the backburner.

The next year I started in a new role and immediately got in touch with our tennis correspondent to ask what he thought about profiling Ward. He thought it was a good idea, but suggested Jamie Baker, a smart former British number two whose career described an arc that would help me ask the questions I was interested in, about how hard it is to keep going when you know how good you are and the world does not. I contacted the Lawn Tennis

Association and pitched the idea. They liked it too, and promised to raise it with Baker at their next meeting. A few weeks rolled past; I nudged them again; they promised to raise it again, the following Saturday. That Saturday afternoon I looked at the BBC Sport website and saw a story headlined 'Jamie Baker retires from tennis aged 26'.

This was not wonderful news for my vision of following him to tournaments in Dubrovnik and Dundee. But, after a bit of thought, I concluded that the piece would still be worth doing, if Baker was sufficiently interested to give me a great deal of his time, and sufficiently thoughtful and articulate to fill me in on the stuff I had missed.

The first time I sat down with Baker, he dispelled my doubts at once, talking passionately about the weirdness of tennis's professional structure, and laying bare his insecurities about his future outside of the game. He knew what I was getting at. I often think that's another way you can tell a good idea from the bad: when you have a bad idea, you have to explain it, again and again, to every interviewee, who only see the point you're making at the second or third attempt. With a good one, they get it right away – and often they've already thought about it.

It wasn't how I planned it. Instead of following Baker to far-flung corners of the earth, I followed him to his new job at HSBC; instead of watching him at Wimbledon, I talked to him for hours, and watched the players who might be his successors in Loughborough. But in the end, I think the piece worked. Here are a few things it taught me:

- Look out for stories in the stuff you're just thinking about. When you spot a story by someone else and think 'Why didn't I think of that?', the infuriation is usually mostly because actually you did think of it – you just didn't recognise it as a story idea. Try to remember that on the tube and in bed and at the movies, you might be working without realising. Make notes on your phone when things strike you. This is surprisingly hard, but it's a habit, and it gets easier.
- So many of the best stories, in all fields, are found at the margins. Roger Federer has been written about endlessly and unless you're in very unusual circumstances you will have no access. Also, he's a seasoned media practitioner, and he doesn't often come out with stuff that will give you a deep insight into his soul. Talking to Baker, in contrast, was more like talking to a friend. I never had to deal with a press officer after the initial contact. And to me, the story of someone talented but not extraterrestrial, struggling to make the most of his gift, is far more compelling than the story of the genius. The same things hold true in music, in botany, in politics … in everything.

(Continued)

(Continued)

- Don't feel that every idea has to arise from a specific person or event – sometimes you can notice a general phenomenon and then find a good example, so long as you're flexible about how you're going to tell your story.
- For a major feature, be prepared to do a lot of reporting and research before you commit to writing the piece – this may seem like a waste of time but it's better than getting halfway through and finding the material isn't good enough.
- If you're new to a subject, pick the brains of as many people as possible – including other journalists, who usually don't deserve their reputation for brutal competitiveness – they will often be enormously helpful. (And you should help other people out too!)

7   The magazine example

Let's look at one specific magazine and see how it could provide inspiration for your own features. I have chosen an issue of *Stylist* magazine from 17 September 2014.

Here is a list of everything it has in it, and the feature ideas they made me think of. As with all of the ideas throughout this book, I have tried to write them as they come to me and not edit them for quality – remember, not all of your ideas will be good enough to make it to pitching stage, the point is to learn how to have so many ideas that you will always have some good ones to choose from.

Extra wraparound cover – advert for Aldo shoe shop. The model is wearing lace-up shoes and '#PERFECTPAIR' is written across her picture. On the inside front page of the extra cover is another model, this time wearing sparkly trainers, with the same hashtag.

- Does the increased use of hashtags make people who don't use Twitter feel alienated?
- Lace-up boots are fashionable again – a look, with diagrams, at the different ways to thread shoelaces.
- People talk about their favourite pair of shoes.
- How to treat shoes well so that they last a lifetime.
- How many pairs of shoes does the average person in the UK have – a look in their shoe cupboards.
- Are there any factories in the UK that make shoes? Go and see how shoes are made.
- Is it worth getting a pair of shoes made to measure?

Cover – A picture of the singer Pharrell Williams in a Rodinesque pose headlined 'The Thinker'. He is wearing a striped sports shirt under a purple jacket and three-quarter length yellow trousers, against a background of pastels. His trainers are designed to look as if they are splattered with paint.

- The pastel palette of Pharrell's outfit makes me think of the Pink Stinks campaign around girls' clothes. I have also recently noticed more clothes for boys on the High Street in pink. So I would be interested in doing a round-up of unisex clothes in pink on the High Street and charting the rise of this, and a look at the Pink Stinks campaign and its successes and challenges.

- An article for men on how to inject more colour into your wardrobe.

Double-page spread advert for a perfume, Reveal by Calvin Klein. Shows a man and a woman, semi-naked, embracing. Also includes a hashtag, #REVEALMORE.

- I have read in the past about sessions offering people the chance to design their own perfume at perfumeries. The perfume in this advert looks super packaged and commercial, and gave me the idea of seeking out the opposite and trying to find people who make their own perfumes at home and how they do it.

A single page advert for Belvedere Vodka, featuring a male and female model in party mode, in a decadent room holding their drinks.

- How to tell the differences between types of vodka – perhaps organise a tasting with an expert.
- Cooking with vodka.

Contents page – a picture of three androgynous models in bright tailoring walking down an urban street, and a list of what can be found in the magazine.

- A look at creating a shared wardrobe for male/female partners, perhaps for a holiday. What items can both sexes wear, and would you have to be the same clothes size?
- Androgyny as a deliberate choice – either a historical look at this trend or interviews with people who choose this as their look.

Editor's letter in which the editor recounts a story about Pharrell being interviewed by Oprah and crying when she shows him a montage of people around the world making videos to his song *Happy*, plus a list of who has worked on this issue of the magazine.

- Who are the people who make tribute videos and why? Interviews with them.
- How to make a tribute video that goes viral.
- A history of celebrities crying in public. (Particularly interesting when not part of an apology, and when a man.)

Single-page advert for a NARS lipstick, featuring an arty black and white pose of actor Charlotte Rampling.

- The adverts throughout this issue feature women of varying age ranges and make-up of various prices. Makes me want to write a feature for a publication looking at the range of people who read *Stylist* and how you can produce a magazine that people of all ages are interested in.

The Style List – a spread of 30 different items, including furniture, clothes, make-up and other things, that the magazine is recommending this week. In this issue these include a cushion, a children's book, a leopard-print skirt, a watering can, a red lipstick, a storage unit from Ikea, a lockable box and a pen.

- The ST Dupont pen, costing £77.50, makes me want to find people who use expensive pens and find out the history of their special pens (e.g. they were bought for them as significant presents, or given them after they have been used for momentous events, or they can be regarded as a status symbol).
- Also interested in the people researching how to make better pens – how did they come to be working in this field? Do people go into product design thinking they want to work on pens? And what pen do they use?
- The 'playful mini chest' makes me think of treasure chests and pirates, which leads me down a different path to wondering why we have made pirates into such a big part of children's stories and characters, when actually they are pretty violent and horrible in real life. How have pirates become glamourised?
- The text alongside the red lipstick says 'Made for Virgin Atlantic cabin crew, Glamore Lipstick in Virgin – in it for the long haul' which makes me wonder what other products that we use at home are the result of things being invented for a specific job.
- How changing your lipstick can change your attitude?
- I never go out without lipstick – get someone who always wears lipstick not to wear it for a week.
- What style tips can we take from work uniforms – a look at ideas gleaned from the uniforms or dress codes of different well-known companies and brands.

A single-page advert for a car – the Peugeot 108, that can be personalised in seven ways.

- This, along with the advert for the Vauxhall Adam later in the magazine, suggests there is a trend for allowing people, not just car fans, to personalise how their cars look. A look at some unique bespoke cars and how you can achieve that look, or ideas for personalising your own car (e.g. have seen magnetic patterns in the past that can be attached to the outside of your car door).

A short interview with Laura Carmichael, an actor in the series *Downton Abbey.*

- One of the answers given by Laura is, when talking about her friendship with one of her fellow actors: 'She's mean to me on the show, but in real life we chat and chat, especially about the storylines, partly because we can't talk to anyone else about them!'. This leads to an idea about how professionals keep secrets – not just actors talking about scripts, but also doctors, spies, teachers, beauty therapists, etc. What are some techniques we can all use to make us better at keeping secrets?

Page 12 – A playwright's list of five plays to add to your bucket list and an ad for a *Stylist* magazine event to meet the author of the book *One Day*, David Nicholls, and get a copy of his new book, *Us.*

- In this section playwright Laura Wade lists her favourite plays and she says, 'In my opinion Caryl Churchill is our greatest living playwright ...'. This leads to the idea of a feature looking at our greatest living person in many categories – greatest living engineer, greatest living actor, greatest living hairdresser, etc.
- Also made me think about how playwrights today go about their work. Would like to follow a play from conception to performance, reporting on the writing stage and read-throughs and rehearsals, etc. Could perhaps be done in conjunction with a theatre and their new playwright schemes.

A single-page ad for a range of haircare products that help with thinning hair.

- A scientific look at thinning hair in women and what can be done about it.

Single-page ad for Rimmel lip gloss, featuring Kate Moss.

- This ad, with a red lip gloss featured, combined with many other ads for red lipsticks throughout the magazine, made me wonder about how to find the perfect shade of red lipstick. Would like to do this with some beauty experts and comparison pictures.
- Also interested in people who find their 'signature' shade and stick with it throughout their lives. Perhaps find some older women who can talk about how they found their shade and show pictures of them wearing it at different stages in their lives.

Page 15 – a fashion round-up page from New York Fashion Week, with lots of pictures of models from the catwalk and picking out key trends and figures.

One of texts picks out a model to focus on. It says, 'Kendall Jenner, the chicest Kardashian ...'.

- And what I have been wondering for ages is, who are the Kardashians? I know roughly how they are famous, and I know one is married to the pop star Kanye West, but that is it. Kardashian fever passed me by somewhat. I would like an explainer feature exploring who the Kardashians are, what each one does, how they are connected to each other, the main scandals, etc. surrounding each one, and so on.
- Also, I heard someone on the radio call the Mitford sisters the Kardashians of their day. This made me wonder, who are other people's equivalents from different times – the Richard Branson of the 1930s? The Miley Cyrus of the 1940s? The Duchess of Cambridge of the 1950s? The Brian Cox of the 1960s? The Benedict Cumberbatch of the 1970s? And so on.

Page 16 – A head-to-head political debate section – a politician on each side of the Scottish Independence debate each gives five reasons to support their case.

- In countries that have gained independence, what happened to families and friendships and relationships. Would find case studies from these and match the demographic to publications to offer case study based stories (e.g. teenagers talking about friendship to a teenage magazine).
- Also interested in finding someone who has lived in the same place all their life but under the rule of different countries and how things changed under each regime.

Single-page ad for 'Idealia Life Serum' which, according to the ad, 'Helps transform the appearance of skin exposed to stress, pollution or a busy lifestyle'.

- I find the whole idea of this product laughable and keep asking myself what is it really for. Would like to either take this seriously and get beauty experts to explain what products with equally mystifying descriptions are for, or to ask people who use them what they think they are for and whether they work.

Two double-page spreads for Marks and Spencer, the first focusing on its 'Luxury Leather' range and the second on its 'Fabulous Folklore' range.

- Interested in people who work as tanners. Also, leather coats as investment pieces. How to choose good quality leather? How to recycle leather?

Page 22 – Elsewhere section – 'Bitesize world news in one helpful page'. This issue features snippets of news from the United States, Japan, China, Brazil, Singapore and Austria (e.g. the story from Austria is about a woman in the Austrian town of Baden going about her daily life naked except for a pair of trainers, and the story from the United States is about a rock group made up of two Hasidic Jewish women who perform women-only gigs).

- Interested in the world of religious pop and rock music. Who are the bands? Who are the fans? Do any ever make it into the mainstream (do they want to)?

Single-page ad for Gap, featuring a woman lounging on a chair in a white top and black trousers and the line 'black is a colour'.

- No ideas from this.

Single-page ad for the shop Wallis, featuring a model in a black knitted jumper. No information other than the shop's name and website address.

- No ideas from this.

Page 25 – Careers section, featuring a day-in-the-life interview with Joanna Geary, Head of News at Twitter UK.

- Interested in how Twitter has changed people's working lives. Would like to interview people in different jobs about life before Twitter and life after Twitter (e.g. police forces often tweet about their day – how has this changed the job of the communications team?). Would be interesting for a publication aimed at people working in communications and for a general one.
- Also read a statistic some time ago about how a high proportion of the jobs our children will do haven't been invented yet. Would like to look forward at what some of these jobs might be. Also talk to older people about some newly invented jobs and see if they can guess what they involve. See if there are any case studies of older people doing these jobs. Then flip it and see whether people newly entering the jobs market can guess what jobs from 50 years ago involved.

Single-page ad for the drink Tia Maria, featuring a woman leaning seductively against a bar looking at a man that we can just see a little of from behind, with the slogan 'Silence speaks louder than words' and the hashtag #InTiaWeTrust.

- It would never cross my mind to have Tia Maria. Leads to idea for an article about what drinks we might like if we tried them, along the lines of 'If you like this then you might also like ...'. Also a guide to when drinks are traditionally drunk (e.g. what is for before dinner, what for after, etc.).

Page 27 – A travel section with a feature spread over two pages looking at three city-centre havens in London, each hotel catering to a different budget.

- Using the idea developed earlier in this book that if you change the subject, angle or audience you have a whole new feature idea, I would be interested in looking at havens other than hotels (e.g. parks, spas, hidden away plazas, etc., and also transferring this idea to other cities).

A single-page ad for the homeware and furniture shop Habitat, featuring a scene of a family relaxing and playing in a living room.

- On the floor in the image, hard to see as it is tucked away beside a large toy giraffe, is a Rubik's Cube. I was in a museum recently that had an exhibition of toys including the book on how to solve Rubik's Cube, written by a teenage maths genius, that I then went and bought on eBay. Am interested in what happened to the writer next. And which toys from the same era did and didn't make it. And recollections of the Rubik's Cube if I can find a good hook.

A single-page ad for the ice cream Häagen-Dazs (it's a black and white picture of a man and a woman smooching with the strapline 'Attraction can't be faked' and lower down the page, 'Neither can our strawberries').

- Interesting ice cream flavours to make at home.
- Alternatives to ice cream.
- How to make old ice cream favourites (e.g. knickerbocker glories or banana splits).
- Foods to spice up your sex life.

Page 31 – A column from the journalist Lucy Mangan, about how nice it is to play the expert when you have a child before your friend.

- Things I have learned since becoming a mother.
- How friendships change when you have children and your friends don't.

A double-page spread advert for the Woody Allen film *Magic in the Moonlight*.

- In the light of paedophilia accusations, is it okay to watch Woody Allen films?

A single-page ad for a new drink in the Coca Cola range, Coca-Cola Life, which, says the ad, has sweetness from natural sources and is lower in calories. The ad shows a bottle of the drink in a meadow, and it has a green label.

- The greenification of fake foods.
- What's really in your fizzy drinks?
- How to make your own alternative to fizzy drinks (e.g. homemade lemonade).

Page 35 – a fashion page with a large picture of a new leather rucksack from Whistles, and some accompanying text.

- In the age of bags as fashion accessories, a look at people who have owned their bags for a long time and why they love their bag.

A nine-page fashion spread, as highlighted in the picture used for this issue's contents page, 'Fine figure', featuring androgynous models in colourful tailoring – 'Zoot-suit swagger meets feminine cool in this season's sharp tailoring and bold colours'.

- Interviews with deliberately androgynous people.
- How to buy a suit.

Advertorial page with a reader discount for Marks and Spencer, featuring another androgynous model in a tailored suit and smart coat.

- No ideas from this.

Double-page ad featuring the actress Blake Lively on one side and a picture and information about the product, a 'perk-up cream' on the other, by L'Oréal.

- A test feature looking at whether perk-up products work.
- A look behind the scenes at the branding of these products – who are the people who come up with the concept, the recipe, the branding?

A three-page feature including a full-page shot of the model Pam Lucas, aged 65. The feature is headlined 'How do you feel when you look at this woman?' and is about the pro-ageing movement, younger women who are embracing the ageing process. It includes a box of six skincare products that 'work wonders for women of any age'.

- All very well for these beautiful, healthy or active older women, but what is life like if you are none of these? Why can't we be honest about what being older can be like?

- 65 is not old – what about women in their eighties and nineties?
- Intergenerational friendships – what are they like and can they ever be equal? Are mothers jealous of their daughters' friendships with women of their mothers' age and vice versa?

A single-page ad from John Frieda and Boots for the Brilliant Brunette haircare range.

- Whether hair products aimed at specific hair colours work and, if so, how?

A single-page ad from Boots for the Luster Pro Light Teeth Whitening System.

- How teeth whitening works.
- Common oral health problems and solutions.
- Who are the people who want to become dentists – why?

Page 53 – a beauty page with a feature on 'Has Kenzo just reinvented winged eyeliner?'

- Other old-fashioned make up styles that are due a comeback?
- Let women's grandmothers do their make up for them and vice versa and have a photo-led feature on the results.

Page 54 – a beauty page – featuring six recommended products with pictures.

- Some of these products are very expensive (e.g. Blue Diamond Super-Cream by Omorovicza £275) – are there products that can be bought as an investment? What are they?

Single-page ad from Tesco and Optrex for the Eye Revive Range.

- How to look after your eyes.

A four-page interview with cover star Pharrell Williams.

- Loads of ideas from this article as it covers so much, but I am particularly interested in a separate box on male feminists. This could be explored much further (e.g. talk to groups of men of different ages about whether they are feminists).

(In the middle of the previous article), a single-page ad for BHS, focusing on a specific pair of black trousers and a red coat and red high heel shoes.

- The resurrection of BHS – how did it go from being dowdy to being fashionable?
- I used to have a Saturday job in BHS when I was a teenager and this ad has made me think about people's Saturday jobs and an article looking at their recollections of them. Wonder if I could find case studies of people who have worked in the same place at different times to see how things have changed – could focus on fashion, or employment practices, etc.

Another single-page ad for BHS focusing on a specific dress and bag.

- As above.

A four-page feature called 'Could there be a better sitcom?' looking at the phenomenon of *Friends*. Includes a box of ten things you never knew about *Friends*.

- A look at other sitcoms from the era (e.g. get an 18-year-old now to watch *Sex and the City* and give their response to it (I was 18 when it I first saw it). How dated is it?

In the middle of the above feature, a single-page ad from Starbucks focusing on Origin Espresso.

- How do people make their coffee at home? Lots of case studies. Tips from top baristas. A product round-up of what you need to make good coffee at home.

Advertorial for Coca-Cola Life – 'To celebrate the launch of Coca-Cola Life, *Stylist* suggests other ways to enhance your precious lunch hour'.

- Things to do in your lunch hour to change your life (e.g. write for half an hour, go for a run, volunteer, trade shares, etc.).

Single-page ad for Regenerate 'advanced toothpaste'.

- What is in toothpaste? How does it work?
- What toothpaste do dentists use? (Similarly for other jobs, e.g. what shampoo do hairdressers use?)
- Is there any truth that putting toothpaste on your spots helps to get rid of them, and other beauty myths.

A three-page feature (first page is just a picture and headline and standfirst) 'Why I became a temporary wife' about a woman who fell in love in Iran.

- A look at other relationships across cultures, not just involving lovers but also mothers-in-law and daughters-in-law or sons-in-law, siblings bought up in different countries, grandparents and grandchildren in different countries. Needs strong case studies.

In the middle of the above feature, a full-page job recruitment advert for the police.

- What life is really like for a female police officer?
- The ad has ways to follow the police via social media. How are the police using this innovatively? (As an example, police helicopters have Twitter feeds.)

Single-page ad for a car, a Vauxhall Adam. Slogan – 'As individual as you are'.

- Personalised cars as per Peugeot ad above.
- Who names cars and how?

One-page advertorial for Gallo wine featuring the model and DJ Amber Le Bon.

- How do we choose which wine to buy? Spend an evening in the wine aisle of a supermarket. Ask people why they are buying what they are buying? Is it branding or price or something else? How much do they know about wine?

Single-page ad for *Emerald Street*, the free daily email from the magazine. It is a picture of some breakfast pancakes with blueberries, and headlined 'Who doesn't love brunch?' and goes on to say, 'Nobody we know. Enjoy exclusive deals on our favourite meal at emaraldstreet. com/brunch'.

- Great brunch ideas to cook at home.
- Where to go for brunch?
- Other combination meals (e.g. afternoon tea and dinner could become a new phenomenon piece on 'afternoon dinner').

Single-page ad for the film *The Riot Club*.

- This ad highlights three reviews, two giving four stars and one giving five stars. A look into how this works, talking to lots of reviewers – how do they decide how many stars to award? Are they influenced by the chance to appear on a poster? Is there consistency? Bribery?

Page 77 – listings page with ideas for going out, including theatre, comedy, music, art and a food festival.

- One of the listings is for a comedy show 'Stand up for ugly animals' in which comedians showcase and defend the world's weirdest animals. But what about a genuine article looking at less cute animals and how to get them the same attention as tigers, pandas and other cute animals. Does anyone care about saving a weird beetle, for example? Who are the people who spend their lives working with ugly animals?

Single-page ad for East Village London, suggesting readers rent a home in the former Athletes' Village in the Olympic Park, which is five minutes from the shopping centre Westfield.

- Shopping holidays in the UK – where to stay, what to buy, how to get there, etc.?
- A tour around the Olympic village now.
- What's happened to other Olympic villages around the world?

Page 79 – literature page – a feature that sets two books on a theme against each other and declares one of them a winner. This week two writers review *Comptoir Libanais Express* by Tony Kitous and Dan Lepard and *Plenty More* by Yotam Ottolenghi.

- My favourite recipe books feature – from normal people, from famous people, from cooks?
- If you could only have three (or five, or ten, or another amount) cookery books, what should they be?
- Ideas for making books of family recipes to be handed down the generations.
- What are the must-haves in countries around the world? Who, for example, is the Greek Nigella, or the Nigerian Jamie?

Single-page ad for the film *Wish I Was Here*.

- One of the characters pictured in the ad has pink hair. I've noticed lots of people recently with brightly coloured hair – would like to find out why they do this? Attention seeking? Fashion statement? Sometimes they have bad roots – so not necessarily a vanity thing. Is it odd to take the trouble to dye hair but not maintain it? Are these shy people hiding behind brightly coloured hair, or show-offs?

Page 81 – cinema page – a page of reviews of recent releases and also a plug for a nationwide screening on a specific date for a broadcast of a live performance of *Billy Elliot The Musical*.

- Why would you want to see a live performance streamed in a cinema? What's the point? Go and see it and work out what the advantage is? How does it compare to being at the real thing?

Single-page ad for Marks and Spencer 'New Taste Collection' food, featuring their new Thai Chicken Penang with Sticky Jasmine Rice.

- What to order next time you go for Thai – understanding the menu. Could be done for all nationalities (e.g. What you need to know before ordering Thai, Indian, Chinese, Vietnamese, etc., such as what the main styles of cooking are, what the main ingredients are, etc.).

Page 83 – a food page, with a recipe for Spiced Dorset Apple Traybake and an advertorial column for a Bourjois red lipstick.

- A cake map of the country – which cakes come from where? What is the defining feature of each one?

Page 84 – celebrity page, a regular feature called 'Queen of Everything' in which a celebrity talks about what she would do if she was in charge of the world. This issue features the actor Maggie Wheeler.

- A look at actors who did make the move into politics. A serious article looking at how this worked out.
- She says in the interview that she co-directs a community choir. A look at how to set one up. All the things to consider (e.g. should it be open to everyone or do you need auditions).

Inside back cover and back cover are part of the extra wraparound cover that is the Aldo ad, one featuring a model in a pair of over-knee boots and the one on the back featuring a model in very high heels with the main bit of the shoe in black with a red heel.

- How comfortable are over-knee boots? How to wear them. How to keep them nice.

Of course, anyone else going through this magazine may pick out different things. They may, for example, notice that the model on the extra front cover has huge question mark earrings or a spotty blouse or gold bangles. They might notice Pharrell's tattoo instead of his trainers. That is why this kind or exercise can be so good for coming up with ideas – no two people will be inspired in the same way by every piece, so you are bound to come up with some new ideas of your own.

You may also have noticed that the ideas I have given are mostly just subjects and angles – they need an audience to be a proper idea. Which means that each idea could be applied to several different audiences and make many articles.

Task: Dissect a publication

Go through any publication making a list of what is on each page. See if you can come up with at least one feature idea from each advert, article or section.

---

8 Getting ideas from people you don't know, places you've not been and things you haven't done before

You don't just get ideas from people you know. Look at the person sitting opposite you next time you are on a train. You don't know this person but you should be able to generate multiple ideas just by looking at them. For example, you might notice that the person is wearing clothes from high street brands but a very expensive watch. You would then ask yourself questions about this, such as why there is the discrepancy between clothes and accessory and how you can tell it is an expensive watch. Or you might ask yourself where this person is going and why. It doesn't matter whether your guesses are correct or not if they lead you to interesting ideas for articles – the person you are looking at is your temporary muse, but they will never know it and therefore it is the ideas here that matter and not the truth.

On the train to my office on the morning I sat down to write this chapter, I was sitting opposite three women who were travelling separately. Each looked very different and, rather oddly, each was picking at their fingernails. All three of them had painted fingernails – one had baby blue varnish, one had conventional pink varnish and another had dark purple varnish. As you can imagine this led to some ideas:

- Are bad habits contagious (e.g. if someone sitting next to us is picking their fingernails (or picking their nose or farting, etc.) are we more likely to do it too? A look at the psychology of picking up bad habits.
- Are your fingernails letting you down? You dress smartly, have expensive haircuts and a designer bag, but you always ignore your nails. An article for professional women about how nails can complete or destroy a look?
- A guide to modern nail decoration techniques?
- Will fingernail painting for men ever catch on – for a men's magazine, take five men for fancy manicures, fake nails or interesting shades of polish and see how this affects their lives – are they taken seriously? Does it stop them typing quickly? Do people assume they are cross-dressers? Does anyone find it sexy? And so on.
- A day in the life of a nail technician.
- What your nail decoration says about you.
- How to rescue weak nails? What to eat? What creams to use? When to see a doctor? And so on.

Let's say you see a person on the bus (or if you persist in not leaving your desk, a picture of someone online) and they are wearing a military style jacket. You might be inspired to think about why this has become popular or which groups in society embrace this style (ironically often peace protestors or anarchists). Perhaps you will look at different military uniforms around the world or world leaders that have inspired fashions (Mao, Nehru, etc.). Maybe you will look at how uniforms have changed over the years or the interesting materials used in uniforms (which in turn becomes an object, as per Chapter 2, and you can then apply the technique described there). Maybe you will be inspired to think about how you react when you see someone in uniform (do you find it sexy, scary, intriguing?) and how this differs around the world (some inspire awe, some fear, some indifference, etc.). Or perhaps you will come up with a feature looking at where to buy military-inspired clothing or real army surplus clothing. Perhaps you will explore the link between military-style uniforms and fascism or go and spend a day at the factory that makes army fatigues.

Once you get into this mindset there are limitless questions to ask and ideas to be had.

Don't restrict yourself only to people who look 'interesting'. If someone looks conventional ask yourself what it is that makes them look conventional. If they are wearing a yellow jumper and you have not seen anyone else in a yellow jumper that week ask yourself why – are they unfashionable or on the cutting edge of fashion? What statement is the person making? Even no statement is a statement of wanting to fit in.

As I sit down to write this section, I can see one other person. He is wearing a Team GB t-shirt from the 2012 Olympics (I am writing this in 2014). This makes me think of lots of questions that could lead to potential feature ideas. How many were bought? Will they still be being worn at the next Olympics? In ten years' time? In 50 years' time? What do you think when someone with a non-athletic build is wearing a sporty outfit? When does a previously fashionable item become unfashionable? When does it become 'retro'? What clothing is best to wear to participate in sport? And to watch sport? Are there any psychological studies looking at whether wearing sportswear makes you more active? And so on.

Remember, it is not just clothes that make up how someone looks. Take in their hair and make-up, their jewellery and shoes, their bags, watch and umbrella. What about their nails? Does their skin look healthy? Do they have wrinkles? Are they wearing glasses? Are their eyes the same colour? Do their socks match? Does the person look happy and what tells you the answer to this? Where do you think they are going and why?

Also, remember to look for incongruous details – the person with scruffy clothes but an expensive watch, neat make-up on their face but chipped nail polish, women's clothing but a prominent Adam's apple, a business suit but a skull-and-crossbones ring, clothes that look too old for them or too young. This could lead to all kinds of feature ideas, from trying to live for a year only buying your clothes in charity shops to swapping outfits with your mum for a week or letting your partner choose what you wear.

Basically, be inquisitive. You are effectively a detective trying to work out what stories these visual clues may lead to. Some of these will make you think 'that's interesting' and those are the ones that will lead to feature ideas.

You may want to develop a list of questions you can work through in your head whenever you are bored and can find someone to use as your secret muse. Such as:

- Where are they going?
- What do they do for a living?
- Do they always dress like that?
- What will they have for dinner tonight?

Also have a list of questions you ask people you meet from any industry:

- What is the most interesting fact about your profession?
- What are you always asked at parties?
- What don't most people know about what you do?
- What is the most expensive tool you use?
- What do you always carry with you to a job?
- Do you find these questions annoying?

Task: Follow someone around

Do a day's work shadowing, ideally in a job you haven't done before. Ask someone if you can watch them at work for the day, or follow them around. You want to be an observer not an active participant, so don't ask for work to do. Instead, watch and take notes, and ask questions when you can.

This doesn't have to be an 'exciting' job. You should get ideas from watching an accountant at work just as you would if you were following a police officer around for a day.

At every step of the way ask yourself (or them, if you feel able) why they are doing what they are doing, why they are doing it that way, what they hope to achieve from it, what problems are likely to arise, whether they think it could be done in a better way and any other questions you think may lead to interesting answers.

If you are particularly interested in a specific industry or subject, try to shadow more than one person (e.g. several different roles in a school or hospital, or several roles in a law firm from secretary up to senior partner).

(Continued)

(Continued)

Alternatively, choose a job. Think of all the questions you would ask someone who did that job, if you were allowed to ask them anything at all. See what ideas this leads to. If you're stuck, here are some ideas to get you started:

- A zookeeper – what do you want to know about their day or the animals they work with?
- A soldier – what do you want to know about their emotions and fears, or their family life?
- An undertaker – what do you want to know about death and burials?

Tip: Me, me, me

All articles boil down to being about people, even though this may not be obvious at first. The article may be about the properties of a newly discovered metal or how to cook a particular meal or the mating habits of squirrels, but at the heart of it, even if just implicit, is the impact of this on people, be it things we need to know about our world or a lesson we need to learn about the world, or how other people do things. As such, always ask yourself, what does this mean for me?

Even the dullest person you know has something interesting about them, even if it why they are so boring.

I was once talking to a dentist at a work party. In theory, dentists should have loads of stories, and I have loads I would like to ask a dentist. I want to know how good their own teeth are and what brand of toothpaste they use at home, whether they ever feel sick at the sight of someone's mouth and how often they come across bad breath, what the worst thing you can eat for your teeth is and whether they are analysing your teeth while they talk to you, whether they know if a patient is lying to them about how much they floss and whether they ever get bored of teeth. Whether they tell their own children about the tooth fairy and how much money they leave them for a tooth. Whether they hire surly receptionists on purpose and why so many dentists' waiting rooms are uninviting. I want to know what made them so interested in teeth and health that they became dentists and whether it was a toss-up between, say, eyes and teeth, and they could easily have been an optician instead. I'd like to know whether, if you can be a human dentist, you could equally well be an animal dentist, and what they make of people with gold teeth. Whether gappy teeth make them want to start recommending braces to adults and whether their minds ever drift while performing dental surgery. How they put people who are scared of the dentist at ease and whether they are privately contemptuous of such a fear. And that's just the beginning…

This particular dentist was not very forthcoming with information. He didn't really like being questioned, especially about the less than serious stuff. My conversation with him led to no article ideas about dentists.

It did, however, make me think about people who are reticent about talking about their work and how they deflect conversations and wonder whether there could be a feature article in that. And it also make me think about people who can't talk about their work for some reason (e.g. spies), and how they deal with that. Also, what it might like to be married to, or the child of, someone who can't talk about their work. See, even conversations that don't go anywhere can lead to feature ideas.

How to make boring subjects interesting

It is worth flagging up first of all that not everyone finds the same things boring. Your dull-as-dishwater topic may be someone else's dinner party talk of choice. What's more, as a feature writer it is your job to find the points of interest in every subject.

There are several techniques to do this:

- Think 'what's in it for me/what's not in it for me?'. Can lessons from what you are writing about be applied to your readers' lives?
- Apply the 'toddler test' – ask why, why, why? Take the subject down to its basic level and imagine you are trying to explain to a toddler why what you are writing about exists at all. So, you are writing about cricket – imagine telling a toddler about team games, or how cricket developed, or where in the world it is played. And while you do so, imagine this is all new to you too – what questions would you want to ask?
- Think why do people who find this interesting, find it interesting, and then find those people and ask them.
- If you can't work out how to make it interesting, then change your idea. Don't flog a dead horse – if you can't summon up enthusiasm then why would your reader?

Spotting a trend

Common wisdom has it that once is an accident, twice is a coincidence and three times is a trend (or, as Ian Fleming put it in the James Bond book *Goldfinger*, 'Once is happenstance. Twice is coincidence. Three is enemy action.').

Incidentally, the preceding paragraph alone should give you ideas: How do literary quotes become 'common wisdom'? Why isn't the word 'thrice' in common use? What is the best James Bond book? And film? World's spookiest co-incidences, and so on.

For example, as mentioned previously in Chapter 6, I have noticed several ice cream parlours popping up near the area in which I live over the past couple of years. Last week I drove about two miles and spotted three. To me, that indicates a new trend worth exploring, from what flavours are most popular, how they are made and how to replicate them at home to who the clientele is and why ice cream parlours are becoming popular.

I also got a train on a hot day and noticed three men in my carriage combining formal work wear with summer clothes – for example, a suit jacket with surfer shorts and a formal waistcoat over a t-shirt. Not only did it make me smile because it looked ridiculous, but it gave me many ideas for features.

You can, of course, let other people do the trend spotting for you. I read a small piece in London's *Evening Standard* newspaper while writing this chapter, that drew attention to four celebrity couples announcing their engagement in the announcement column of the newspaper *The Times*, with David Mitchell and Victoria Coren doing so in 2012, and Eddie Redmayne, Benedict Cumberbatch and Geri Halliwell all following suit in 2014. I fully expect to read features about the history of announcement columns and ways of telling people you are engaged before I have finished writing this chapter.

Of course, however much you have your ear to the ground and however many newspapers you read, you won't spot every trend and, as the saying goes, once you've spotted the bandwagon you are too late to jump on it. It is worth asking others what trends they have noticed. I am particularly interested in finding out what trends are developing in other parts of the country and other parts of the world. I asked friends living abroad to tell me about any trends they've noticed in their countries, and got the following answers:

- It has gone coffee mad here and now it seems normal to talk about it like wine. Coffee tastings are a thing now here and places where it is almost intimidating to order a cup of coffee have become common. (Australia)
- Thermomixes are a huge craze amongst the suburban middle classes here. (Australia)
- Pelvic floor rehabilitation after childbirth is standard here and they really should do it in the UK. (France)
- Macaroons have definitely caught on here this year, they're everywhere. (Hong Kong)
- There has been a shift from celebrity chefs opening fine dining restaurants to celebrity chefs opening casual dining experiences. Also, food vans seems to be a growing trend, as there are now two with a third coming (which is a big deal here!). It's basically gourmet burgers/other cuisine served from a cool-looking van at the beach, with the location changing sporadically, announced on social media. (Dubai)

- Dried kale chips as snacks for toddlers, Kombucha Tea drinks (for adults) and gel nails ... everyone is wearing them. And I saw a lot of people dress their dogs up in costumes this Halloween. (United States)

Sometimes you may hear about a trend that hasn't yet made it to where you are, in which case you can think about pieces exploring that trend and whether it will make it to where you live. Or if your area has already seen the trend, you can start to look at the global reach (for example, macaroons have been big in the UK for a while – why did the trend take so long to reach Hong Kong?).

Tip: Look for the story behind the story

If, for example, you notice lots of publications using pomegranate seeds in their recipes, go and talk to the pomegranate farmers. How are they meeting demand? What is it replacing? What is happening to the farmers of the product it is replacing? Do pomegranate farmers eat pomegranate themselves?

My story – Ellie Levenson

Ellie Levenson is the author of this book, a freelance journalist and a lecturer in journalism at Goldsmiths College.

The saying goes that if you've spotted a bandwagon then you are too late to jump on it, but if you get wind that something is about to happen then you can appear ahead of the curve by calling for it to happen. Some years ago I knew from my contacts in politics, think tanks and poverty charities that the Labour Government would shortly be introducing a 'Health in Pregnancy' grant, giving all pregnant women, regardless of income, a lump sum once they reached a certain point in their pregnancy. The rationale was that women who can afford to eat more healthily have babies of a healthier birth weight needing less medical care, so there was an economic argument to be made for giving women this money as well as a moral argument. The best way to get this money to women was through a universal benefit so as to cut down on any stigma attached to receiving the benefit, and any administrative hurdles, such as means testing. I thought it was an excellent idea and wrote a feature for the *Guardian* exploring why such a benefit was needed and calling for it to be introduced.

Because Angelina Jolie and Brad Pitt had just had their first biological child at the time, I used this as a hook, saying that although their child would

(Continued)

(Continued)

never want for anything, plenty of children would be born to mothers who can't afford to eat healthily. To be honest, it was quite a tenuous hook – I could have found better statistics or political speeches to use – but the editor liked the celebrity introduction as it meant they could use a big picture of Angelina and Brad alongside the piece. It's quite hard to make stories about benefits, poverty and maternal health 'sexy', so I didn't mind doing this in order to get the issue some attention. The Conservatives/Liberal Democrat coalition subsequently scrapped the benefit, so I imagine there will be scope to write similar articles in the future calling for it to be reintroduced.

As a feature writer you should also perfect the art of listening to people's conversations. I was on the train looking at my iPhone when I overheard two girls opposite me wondering why so many people have iPhones. In their words: 'How come everyone has an iPhone? When did they take over the world?' Great question, and great idea for a feature article. First, have they taken over the world? Or is it just the world the girls and I were in that day (i.e. London or the UK or Europe or the Western world). Also, is this perception borne out through the figures or is it just because iPhones can be easily spotted or because their users are more likely, for whatever reason, to use them in public (as a status symbol? Because their maps are easy to use? Better signal? More likely to be owned by people who check their phones more often? And so on)?

Task: Eavesdrop

Sit in a cafe or pub next to people talking and listen for an hour. Make notes of anything interesting they say to each other that may spark a story idea.

Getting as many articles as you can from your research

You should be able to use the research you've done on one subject to generate several articles. For example, if you have looked into a factory in a developing country that produces lipstick to be sold in Western countries, and where the workers are paid very poor wages, you might be able to develop several ideas such as:

- The real cost of your make-up – an exposé of the industry for a news weekly magazine or a Sunday newspaper.

- The women who make your lipstick but can't afford to wear it – for a women's magazine that includes thoughtful features.
- Is it possible to buy ethical make-up? For the consumer pages of a national newspaper.
- How to create your own make-up – for a website specialising in money saving.

An example of this is an article I wrote for the magazine of the *Financial Times*. I was lecturing as an Associate Professor at the London campus of Syracuse University, an American university based in New York State. I noticed on the wall a tribute to some students who had died in the Pan Am 103 explosion over the town of Lockerbie in Scotland on 21 December 1988. Thirty-five Syracuse students returning from a semester in London were killed in the disaster. With the twentieth anniversary coming up (in 2008), I wrote an article about the continuing links between the Scottish town and the American university. Then, using my contacts in Lockerbie, I wrote a piece for the education section of the *Guardian* about how the school and community in Lockerbie teaches current pupils about the incident, given they hadn't been born at the time, and how to give it resonance without focusing on it to the detriment of more positive things in the town's history. This, in turn, reawakened an interest I have had for a long time in how schoolchildren are taught about difficult episodes of recent history, and I then wrote an article, also for the education section of the *Guardian*, about how schools in the UK teach students about the genocide in Rwanda.

My story – Jenny Wood

Jenny Wood is a freelance journalist and former features editor of *LOOK* magazine.

When it comes to coming up with ideas, you should never really switch off. So, if I'm out shopping and see a fun new product, or at a bar having drinks with friends and spot an unusual new drinking trend, I take a note of it, grab a business card or snap a picture on my phone. Who knows when it might come in useful?

For example, I walked past a gym a while ago which was advertising a new kind of fitness class. I took a note of their number, and asked to speak to whoever dealt with their press enquiries. It turned out that the class I'd seen advertised wasn't particularly interesting; however, they were launching a new 'hangover workout' on weekend mornings that was designed to rid your body of toxins with special exercises, vitamin drinks and being showered with water as you run. It sounded fantastic!

(Continued)

> *(Continued)*
>
> I contacted *Fabulous* magazine – young and trend-led, it comes out on a Sunday with the *Sun* newspaper, making it the ideal place for a feature about beating a hangover. They loved my idea, and sent me and a friend with a photographer to try out one of the very first sessions. The piece was a lot of fun to write, made a double-page spread and has led to more work with the magazine.

Another way to get feature ideas is to think about things you have always wanted to try. This can help in two ways – you might decide to pitch a feature that enables you to try whatever it is you have been wanting to do, be it do a skydive, watch heart surgery, have a kitten for a week, test an extreme diet or meet one of your heroes, or you might decide instead to pitch an article about the people who do these things or enable these things to happen.

If I think about my life now at the time of writing this, here are some things I would like to do:

- I would like to have some lie-ins (my children frequently wake me at 5.30 am).
- I would like to spend some time working in the United States.
- I would like to have a holiday in a camper van or on a canal boat.
- I would like someone else to take over the renovations of my new house so I don't have to worry about it.
- I would like a massage for my shoulders, which are aching as I type this hunched over my computer.

And here are some ideas that have come out of writing that list:

- Things to do in London (or anywhere else) at 5.30 am (as opposed to putting the TV on for the children and hiding my head under a cushion trying to go back to sleep). Could be written for different age groups (e.g. things to at 5.30 am with kids, where to eat out at 5.30 am, etc.).
- Compare places at different times in the day – (what is a park like at 5.30am, 10.30am, 4pm and 10pm?).
- How to make yourself into an early morning person.
- The people who survive on a few hours sleep (e.g. senior politicians, members of the armed forces, pilots, surgeons performing long, complicated surgery, etc.). Look at how they do it and risks involved and whether the brain gets used to it.
- Health implications of too much or too little or broken sleep.
- How to work abroad mid-career (as opposed to casual jobs when younger).

- What I learned from my stint working abroad – either business lessons from a different culture for a business-related publication or a personal piece about cultural lessons learned.
- What jobs in the same industry are like in different countries – either for specialist industry-oriented publications or generalist features (e.g. 'five chefs around the world talk about their work').
- Things you need to know before you holiday in a camper van (or canal boat).
- How to combine your holiday with learning a new skill.
- A history of camper vans – when did people start to sleep in their vehicles? What company first thought of this as a way to sell holidays?
- Lessons you can apply from small living spaces (e.g. camper vans and canal boats) to your own homes (such as good use of storage, no superfluous items, etc.) – for design pages or homes magazines.
- How to brief an interior designer.
- Lessons you can learn from an interior designer.
- Ask an interior designer to come and look at my home and give me pointers and write this up for a piece.
- The benefits of making decisions quickly (either in business, in life generally, in home decoration and so on – probably been some research on this somewhere, definitely worth finding).
- Tools to help you envisage your finished home – if you have trouble imagining what your wallpaper choices will actually look like, here are some ways you can work it out (e.g. make models, computer programmes that help, etc.).
- How to give yourself a massage.
- Massages, breaks and other employer benefits every company should give staff for free.

See, I told you in the introduction to this book that feature writing is an incredibly privileged and enabling job – if I wanted to do these things badly enough, I could probably make them happen by working on these ideas a little more and turning them into pitches (and commissions).

Another good way to get ideas is to go somewhere new. This is both because you need to get out and about every now and then to stay fresh and sane, but also because when you do new things you get new ideas. So go for a walk, and walk down a road you've never been down before, or go to a new exhibition at a gallery. Try a new supermarket or get off at a different bus stop. Or walk the same route you always walk but stop to smell the flowers or read the advertising along the way. Even better, arrange an experience you've been wanting to do – a meal from a cuisine you've never tried before, a historical walking tour, an evening class in silversmithing. If you are a features journalist, no idea is ever wasted.

Tip: Get a different perspective

Think about the same idea from a different perspective. So perhaps an idea about heart surgery might work from the angle of thinking of what it is like to be a patient receiving a new heart. But now think about the doctor and how they feel giving it. Or the donor's family. Or the recipient's spouse, etc.

As well as trying something new specifically to get ideas, you can go to new places, or places you have been to before, and spend some time looking around and taking in all the small details you might usually miss. For example, do you frequently go to a gallery that has ornate carving on the outside? Now is the time to wonder who carved it or how it is maintained. Who made the sign outside your local grocery shop or who chooses which charity collectors are allowed to collect at your local supermarket?

I had a disastrous haircut in an expensive hairdressers recently, so one day I decided on a whim to pop into a branch of a very cheap hairdressers in the shopping mall near my house. In this salon you just turn up and wait your turn for the next available hairdresser rather than book an appointment with a specific person. As this was a place I had never been before, I decided to use the waiting time (about 45 minutes) to look around the salon properly and write down all the thoughts and ideas that came to me from sitting waiting in this place

Here they are:

- Is there any correlation between cut and price when it comes to haircuts? Get people with cheap cuts and people with expensive cuts and ask others to guess which is which?
- Why is it that confident grown-ups are still embarrassed about telling a hairdresser they don't like their cut. How to learn to do this. And get a hairdresser's view on this. Tips from a confidence coach, etc.
- Rules for cutting your own hair – dos and don'ts.
- People talk about their past disastrous haircuts.
- Loud music in salons (and other shops) – whether it drives sales. Impact on staff. Whether it has a negative health/mood impact. (Could link to classical music played in some train stations to influence behaviour.)
- Incongruous music (e.g. beauty therapists playing rap instead of whale music).
- How to utilise dead time (e.g. I am writing this while sitting and waiting in the hairdressers).
- How to be an advert for your business (e.g. hairdressers with bad hair).
- The game my husband and I play sometimes when walking down new streets – guessing from a distance whether a business is a hair salon or a restaurant. Could this be made into a feature in which readers are

invited to guess the same? Or made into a feature about games and in jokes that couples develop.

- A model on a poster on the wall is wearing a peace sign on a necklace. Do people still wear that? It was a cool symbol for my parents' generation and also for mine. Has anything else remained cool across generations?
- The woman next to me had tattooed-on eyebrows – how and why to do this? Is it permanent?
- The shop has no toilet for customers. Is this allowed?
- A breakdown of the costs of a haircut – have seen a similar article doing this for coffee shops. Would like to know how it works for hair (e.g. cost of water, shampoo, labour, etc.).
- How do hairdressing salons choose which products to promote?
- The turn-up-and-queue system seems to be borrowed from barber shops. What other ideas from men's lives could women use? Could be feature for women's magazine – 'How to live life like a man'. Could also do other way round for men on how to live life like a woman.
- The salon is unisex – what other things could or should be unisex but often aren't (e.g. public toilets).

Task: Sit somewhere new

Go and sit somewhere new. Look around. Write down all the ideas that come to you and thoughts you have. Don't worry if they are tangential. Don't censor them or only write down good ideas. Write them all down.

There are loads of things you can do. Go and get an ice cream. Go to a museum. See a film. Watch popular YouTube videos. Go for a coffee with a mate. Go for a coffee alone and eavesdrop. Do some gardening. Just getting out and about can help with ideas. On one journey recently, dropping someone off at the station after a meal out, I spotted three things that would potentially make interesting features:

- A barber shop had a sign on the shop front saying it was part of the British Barbers' Association.
- A construction site had a sign up about the Safe Crane Campaign.
- The bus in front of me had an advert on the back for a local school.

Each of these leads to ideas that could be turned into interesting features:

- Interesting ways to work your way around the world (e.g. could a barber just carry their tools with them and set up shop anywhere?).
- The rise of the old-fashioned style barber shop. A feature looking at which kind of men go to these shops and what the experience is like.

- How to choose your barber shop.
- How to be your own barber – if, for example travelling abroad, with advice from professional barbers.
- Why was a Safe Crane Campaign needed – what crane accidents were there and have they been reduced?
- I have always wanted to go up a tall crane – think about writing an experiential feature based on this.
- I have always wondered how cranes are assembled (and disassembled) on top of tall buildings and would like to write a feature about this too (with good pictures).
- What people working on building sites can do if they feel their environment isn't safe – how to be a whistleblower in these circumstances (e.g. if it's an unsafe crane rather than a safe crane).
- Do adverts for schools make a difference to the number of people applying for a place, and why schools in the state sector even need to do this?
- What life skills should children know by certain ages (e.g. quite essential by a certain age to know how to read a bus route and timetable and pay a fare)?
- What everyday things that we don't pay attention to do children find exciting and how to use this in planning adventures for them (e.g. lots of children have never been on a bus before)?
- School trips that adults remember – is it the big, exotic ones or outings like a local bus trip?

Tip: Ask an expert

James Crabtree is Mumbai Correspondent for the Financial Times.

When I had a brief spell working for *The Economist*, my editor always used to say, 'If you find an expert and hold them up by their ankles, a story will surely fall out of their pockets'.

9 Getting ideas from press releases, and from direct contact with charities and press officers

We've not yet touched on getting feature ideas from press releases, or directly from people working in public relations but, of course, giving ideas to journalists is a large part of their job.

Many feature writers, however, try to steer clear of getting ideas in this way, as they feel that too many people will have been given the same information and therefore their idea will lack originality.

It is a mistake to think like this, because what press releases and events for the press do is present you with the gift of a hook. They also often source experts for you and give you helpful facts and statistics, as well as sometimes presenting you with inspiration for excellent ideas.

There are two extreme ways to approach being given information in this way:

1   To think 'Why is this lying bastard lying to me?' (a phrase attributed to foreign correspondent Louis Heren).
2   To be thrilled that you are being given an idea.

The right way, of course, is to take a healthy dose of advice from each of these. When you are given a story you need to think critically about the information you receive. Remember, public relations officers (or PRs as they are more commonly known) are being paid to represent a client, and it is their best interests they have at heart, not yours. Similarly, press officers, even those working for good causes, promote their own organisation above all others.

This doesn't mean that the stories and information they give you aren't good. Nor does it mean that they are seeking to pull the wool over your eyes all the time. But it does mean that you should look at all information you are given with a healthy dose of scepticism, and seek to corroborate any information you are being given, or at least check that it stands up to scrutiny. For example, you may be given statistics based on a survey. You will need to know who commissioned that survey and how it was carried out before giving the results any credence.

Some questions you should be asking to help you do this include:

1   Who are they working for?
2   What are they trying to achieve with this information?
3   Why are they releasing this information now?

It doesn't matter if the answers to the above are (1) they are working for a lipstick company, (2) they want to sell more lipstick, (3) they've released a new product they want you to buy, as long as you are aware of that while also reading the results of the survey they send you saying that 90 per cent of people think women wearing red lipstick deserve to be paid more money than women who don't.

Using polls – Joe Twyman

Joe Twyman is Head of Political and Social Research at YouGov, a global market research and data company.

People are extraordinarily bad at predicting public opinion. We hear a lot of 'all my friends think this' or 'everyone at works says that' but actually public opinion tends to be more nuanced than that. So, in a lot of cases polling can provide the depth beyond simply headline finding, and also can counteract the expectation that people have for public opinion. So looking closely at what a poll tells you can produce all kinds of interesting angles. They are what the journalist Roy Greenslade calls 'Hey Doris' facts. He means that we, as human beings, are interested in what other people think, and we want to see, at a primeval level, how we fit in the order of things, so if there's an interesting finding it will make people sit up and take notice, and say 'Hey Doris, come and have a look at this'.

An example of a poll we conducted that made interesting features for journalists is one that looked at what people think of men wearing red trousers. We managed to catch a point in time where a lot of people were discussing this – it caught the cultural zeitgeist and provided a context for that. Loads of people were retweeting our data to their friends saying, 'I told you people didn't like these'.

Some time before the horse meat scandal [in which a lot of meat being sold in the UK as being from other animals was found to contain horse meat] we asked a question in one of our polls looking at what meat people would eat if it was served to them in a restaurant. We included horse meat and panda meat in the question. It meant when the horse meat scandal broke we had this data that could be used by journalists.

The reason polling is a good resource is that without the facts to back it up from a survey, it's just an opinion. Most reputable polling agencies have press offices and most press officers will be happy to help you. You do need to be aware there's a lot of bad polling out there however. Bad polling can ruin an article.

Another problem, of course, is that you are rarely the only person being given information in this way. Therefore you need to learn how to get an original idea out of information that many other people are also being given.

To do this, I suggest using some of the techniques spoken about earlier in this book – thinking about how objects or issues might affect different groups of people or have different elements to their story, such as where they are made or what they can be used for.

Of course, what is better than receiving a press release sent to many other people is to be given exclusive information by a PR – that is, information that has been given only to you. This doesn't mean, of course, that you take everything they tell you at face value. As with all journalism, you need to verify facts, get opposing views and try to trace stories back to their source.

The best way to see how journalists and people in PR work together is through real-life examples, so the rest of this chapter is given over to examples from journalists explaining how specific articles came about via their contacts with PRs, and from PRs giving tips on how to get the best out of them.

My story – Johanna Payton

Johanna Payton is a freelance journalist.

I wrote an article for *Easy Living* magazine about when pregnancy over the age of 35 isn't a happy accident. It started life as many features do, meeting with a PR to have coffee.

They had been sending me press releases for a while – quite good, well-written press releases, which always makes a PR stand out for me – and I had replied to a couple of them asking for more information. So I was invited out for a coffee and she talked me through all her clients and one was a pharmaceutical company and they were marketing a mini pill for women over 35, because after a certain age you're advised not to take certain contraceptive pills. On the face of it this didn't seem all that interesting to me but then they mentioned a statistic that made my ears prick up – they said that as many women over 35 have an abortion as women under 16.

I thought that was fascinating and as soon as they gave me the statistic I had a clear idea of how it might work out as a feature and I pitched it to the health section of *Easy Living*. Some older women get pregnant accidentally because they don't take contraception seriously due to reading all the headlines about declining fertility, so I focused on that and did a box out on contraception available for women over 35, listing the different methods and including the information about the contraception that the PR was originally telling me about. It also included anonymous case studies.

My story – Olivia Solon

Olivia Solon is the technology editor at the *Daily Mirror* newspaper and former deputy editor of *Wired* magazine.

I was writing about another topic altogether – open access scientific research – and found myself in a meeting with the PR from GlaxoSmithKline. He alerted me to a major area of investment across the industry: electroceuticals.

These are, essentially, pieces of technology that stimulate our existing nervous system in order to deliver a therapeutic effect – so swapping drugs for tiny devices implanted in the body. On a crude level it's about pacemakers and deep-brain stimulation, but GSK wants to be able to map tiny electrodes to very specific neural circuits throughout the body. Many of the body's organs and functions are regulated through circuits of neurons that communicate through electrical impulses. The theory is that, if you can accurately map the neural signatures of some diseases, you can then stimulate the malfunctioning pathways with tiny electrodes to restore health, without the need for molecular medicines.

When I heard the catchy name they'd given the field, and the fact that they were investing a million dollars in research into the area, I was extremely intrigued. So I set about tracking down and speaking to many researchers in this field to see what they thought of Big Pharma's involvement and how these technologies could help people.

Many of the researchers were in the US and were doing awesome things like trying to recreate the neural signals of people with spinal cord injuries, trying to treat conditions like arthritis and diabetes as well as neuro-psychiatric disorders like Parkinson's and epilepsy.

In this case, the idea came at the end of a meeting with the PR about an entirely separate topic. I have found that when I meet with PR teams, it's often not the story they are trying to pitch that is the one that excites me the most. I now nearly always find myself asking if they have anything else going on that they aren't ready to talk about in a press release – any stuff they are working on in a secret lab? Any plucky employees doing something awesome, even though they aren't one of the 'big names'? This line of questioning often produces quirkier stories that aren't on the main corporate marketing agenda.

It is often tempting to see people working in PR as the enemy, and the relationship as one of Us versus Them. Back to the whole 'Why is this lying bastard lying to me' thing again. But, of course, working relationships are far more nuanced than that. Richard Darlington, who has worked in many communication jobs in government and think tanks, puts it well in the box below, when he talks about the idea of 'co-production'.

From the PR – Richard Darlington

Richard Darlington, Head of News, Institute for Public Policy Research (IPPR).

The relationship between PR and journalism is sometimes presented as a war between people protecting corporate or political interests and truth-seeking, heroic, investigative hacks. But, in reality, PR and journalism have a symbiotic relationship, like the one between crocodiles and the plover birds that clean their teeth. At any point, the journalist could turn on their source, just as the crocodile could eat the bird. But they don't. And that's because most 'news' is not found or uncovered, but 'co-produced'.

I've made a two decade long career out of co-production. First, I meet a journalist, often when they are new in their organisation or have just started a new job. I ask the questions and try to understand the pressures that they are under. What are their deadlines? What times of day or week are the meetings where they decide what they are covering? What kind of stories are they trying to serve up for their boss (everyone's got a boss, even the editor!) – both in terms of content and in terms of format? Essentially, I, as a PR, am interviewing them. You'd be amazed how much of themselves a journalist will share with you in return for a coffee and a screen break. Then I offer up some of the round-shaped pegs that might fit into their round-shaped holes that they've told me about. Then we talk some more about what might work. This is co-production. It takes place face to face and eye to eye in the first instance but it can lead to a lifetime of collaboration as both journalist and PR move from job to job, throughout their career. In the process, you may become friends. But crucially, the collaboration of co-production is about the meeting of self-interest. I scratch your back and you scratch mine. Not in an 'I'll owe you one' kind of way but simultaneously. Every Sunday newspaper journalist wants their byline on that week's splash. Editors of political blogs need a constant stream of content, from guest posts to tip-offs and gossip. Good PRs want their story to splash the Sunday papers and their issues to make the weather in the blogosphere. It's a mutually beneficial collaboration but it only ever works through give and take and finding common ground. The golden rules of co-production (why the crocodile never eats the bird) are:

- A respect for operational discussions – we're both allowed to 'think aloud'. The PR is allowed to withdraw a story idea if they can't get their boss to sign it off. The journalist does their best but can't promise coverage.
- We don't 'do each other over' – there is sufficient trust in the relationship for the PR not to give the same story to a competitor (unless we agree, 'this can go all round') and for the journalist not to mislead the PR on their approach ('this is how we could write it/I'm not going to be able to write it like that').
- No one makes promises that we can't keep and we are both open and honest about where we are coming from and what our vested interests are.

Although Richard Darlington is speaking mainly about political news, the same applies to features. The relationship between PR and journalist is not freely given. As a journalist, you want a good feature as well as a great byline and potentially to uncover the truth and serve justice, or at the very least earn some money and get a lead for another feature. And, as PR, you want to get publicity for whoever is paying you to get them publicity (or in some cases, to avoid publicity). By working together you can sometimes serve both of your interests and create a feature that keeps you all happy, and that readers want to read.

From the PR – Alex Goldup

Alex Goldup is a Director of Third Sector PR, which focuses on the not for profit sector.

For many charities, particularly smaller ones, staffing and resources will be tight and you may find that they are reluctant to spend much time finding and checking out case studies or ploughing through databases unless they have a clear indication of what you want and that they will get something in return.

This isn't always the case – and some might just be happy to see an issue or topic given exposure. Often, however, the more you can offer by way of a mention or 'voice' in an article, the more helpful a charity will be prepared to be.

Charity staff can be very nervous about putting media in touch with their beneficiaries. The welfare and wellbeing of the people they help will be paramount and can sometimes lead to a reluctance on their part to follow up on a request, particularly where there are sensitivities – regardless of the potential publicity benefits for the charity. Concessions, such as offering a 'readback' of an article or, where appropriate, copy approval to a case study, can go a long way towards easing anxieties about putting journalists in touch with beneficiaries.

A common complaint is that journalists will put a press officer or PR representative to work – to track down case histories, for example – and then sit on a story or go quiet for weeks or even months. Often there is a perfectly valid reason – a long lead time perhaps or, for a commissioned writer, an uncommunicative editor who doesn't always let on when an article has been delayed. However, be as transparent as you can. Telling a press officer about your timescales, or alerting them if there are likely to be delays, will leave a good impression and keep you in their good books.

My story – Kate Hilpern

Kate Hilpern is a freelance feature writer.

I write a lot on adoption because I am adopted myself and I also sat on an adoption panel for ten years, helping make recommendations for adoption matches, and I was a volunteer as an intermediary helping with adoption reunions for a charity. Therefore I had built up good contacts with organisations working in the field.

Adoption parties, or activity days, are where hard-to-place children and approved adopters get together to do activities in the hope that they feel a connection to each other. They used to be used a lot in the UK but fell out of favour, and when it became apparent a few years ago that they might be coming back in the UK, the *Guardian* asked me to do an article on them, looking at the pros and cons.

Some time later, once it was clear they were working well, the British Association for Adoption and Fostering (BAAF) decided that, because I understood the adoption process and had worked with looked after children, they trusted me to go to an adoption party and report on it. Up until this point these events had been closed to the media. So I pitched it to the *Independent* because I knew the particular editor I sent it to stays very true to copy and is sensitive to these kinds of issues and it also felt like a good match for the audience.

I went along to an adoption party in Bolton, which was very moving and gave me far more than I could possibly write about. Actually going was a really good way to dispel a lot of the myths about what adoption parties are, which was the reason for the piece.

I showed BAAF the piece before I published it. This isn't usual journalistic process but it was part of the trust between us and I wanted them to fact-check it. A lot of people are very scathing about these parties, accusing them of being beauty pageants and child speed-dating, so it was really important that I didn't let the article backfire.

The editor realised it was complex subject with a lot of myth-busting to do, so even though I ended up going over word length, she printed the whole thing.

From the PR – Dave Smith

Dave Smith is Director of the Boaz Trust, a charity helping destitute asylum seekers in Greater Manchester.

There are two things that journalists often don't understand about getting stories from charities.

First, the tighter the deadline, the less likelihood of getting a response. Large charities will probably be able to respond, and some will have some stories on tap, but for the smaller charity, where they are busy fire-fighting and engaging directly with vulnerable people, there is no way they can take time out to go searching for a story, getting in touch with the beneficiary and getting them to agree to do it – especially if it's got a really short deadline

(Continued)

(Continued)

Second, the more open-ended the request, the more likely it is you will get a good story. I get tired of very specific requests for females aged 20 to 35, and even more fed up with requests for stories about people who volunteer over Christmas as I think why portray people giving up one day (sometimes to salve their conscience) as some sort of hero when, if they are serious about helping vulnerable people, they can volunteer the other days of the year, when there is far less provision available. But if you simply ask me 'Have you got a good story?' then I could probably find you half a dozen – in good time.

From the PR – Caroline Hampden-White

Caroline Hampden-White is Head of External Affairs at Children with Cancer UK, a charity that raises money to fund scientific research and welfare projects to help children with cancer and their families.

There's a difference between stories we're 'selling in' and stories that come from the journalist and they then approach us for help. However, with a professional relationship and a good understanding of each other's boundaries you can get some really good stories from both perspectives.

We were working with a freelancer who was looking to do a story about some of our patient representatives (children or teenagers who have been affected by childhood cancer – either a child who is going through or has come out the other end of childhood cancer). We have a bank of case studies of people who have shared their story with us very kindly because they know that will help us to raise awareness of the disease area that we represent.

For example, we had a case study of a young girl called Bethan who had lost most of her hair during chemotherapy. Some children lose their hair and some don't. We were talking about her and the cancer and how it had affected the growth of her bones and the operation she had to take out her arm bones, irradiate them and put them back. But what the journalist was actually interested in was her loss of self confidence through the loss of her hair. So this led the journalist to investigate an article looking at how little girls with long hair are cutting off their hair and donating it to charity so that wigs can be made for children going through cancer treatment, and Bethan was included in the piece as a case study. The angle there was that the youth of today are not as selfish as you might think.

The piece was good for us because it highlighted one of the side effects of a childhood cancer diagnosis, which is this lessened self-confidence, though we only got a small mention at the end of the article and would have appreciated a bit more.

We don't have enormous resources. So we are very happy to help with things that journalists often can't do, such as provide case studies and prepare them according to what a journalist wants and needs, but we don't have the resources to pitch that much so it is really useful if journalists come to us with any kind of semi-relevant ideas and we'll always try to help.

In fact, even if the work of the charity is tangential to your story, do get in touch. I recently did a piece on radio and whilst I couldn't comment on the individual case study they were discussing, I was able to contribute facts and statistics and human interest stories at very short notice.

We can also help journalists to find a hook or an angle for a story. If they have a general idea, we will research things for them and come back with suggestions, such as recent research, projects we've funded, new statistics that have been published, disease trends, etc.

In terms of what we are looking for, we would like three things:

1   wherever possible we're looking for a name check and a website mention
2   we want to highlight the work of the charity
3   we're looking to highlight particular campaigns, for example Childhood Cancer Awareness Month in September.

My story – Hannah Prevett

Hannah Prevett is a freelance journalist.

Growing up in Colchester, a garrison town, meant I was always fascinated with the lives of the soldiers who slept in the barracks and stood at the gates with guns. I frequently wondered what these guys and girls would do if they ever put down the rifle. Every other cab driver seemed to be ex-military.

Thirteen years after leaving Colchester, I attended a networking event for HR directors of big City institutions. The keynote speaker was by Tony Harris, a former officer in the army. He gave an inspirational speech about his road to recovery – he's an amputee – and declared that ex-military personnel made excellent employees. He also mentioned that Jaguar Land Rover had hired 100 such recruits in the last year.

I got in touch with the Jaguar Land Rover press office, who were very accommodating and arranged for me to have a tour of the Solihull plant, where I would also meet with two ex-services personnel. It was a great day and I got a real insight into how these people's lives had changed on 'civvy street'. One woman told me that she kept expecting to get a tap on the shoulder and to be sent overseas again.

(Continued)

(Continued)

I realised that I wanted to speak to people at all levels of seniority within the military so I also interviewed a partner at PricewaterhouseCoopers (PwC), the consultancy firm, who was formerly second in command of a thousand-strong parachute regiment and then equerry (military secretary) to the Prince of Wales and the Duchess of Cornwall. I gathered additional input from the Career Transitions Partnership, which works with soldiers on resettlement.

This feature appeared in the *Sunday Times*. I hope to write another article in the future with Jaguar Land Rover, as they are launching a programme helping to rehabilitate wounded servicemen and women. I will definitely follow up as I found it deeply fulfilling writing this piece. My strongest articles are always on a subject I'm truly passionate about – though they're also the most stressful to write as you're desperate to do them justice.

From the PR – Malcolm Clark

Malcolm Clark is the former co-ordinator of Make Votes Count and is currently co-ordinator of the Children's Food Campaign.

It can pay dividends, when you spot a relevant story in the news, to do some extra research that you can offer journalists in order to help with follow-up stories and features.

For example, a couple of days after the second or third wave of stories in the *Daily Telegraph* during the MPs' expenses scandal, I spotted a post by a friendly amateur politico, Mark Thompson, who had done some number-crunching on his blog, Mark Reckons, to correlate the MPs embroiled in the scandal with the size of their majority. He found the vast majority were in what might be considered to be safe seats. I immediately saw the usefulness this could have for our campaign for proportional representation. I contacted the blogger and worked with him over the weekend to make the statistical analysis more rigorous and to write an accompanying piece explaining the links with the need for electoral reform. I then reblogged his piece on the Make Votes Count site, and started contacting some friendly journalists and bloggers with our research.

Sure enough, it was picked up. By the Thursday, the stats and link were recited live on BBC *Question Time* by a Labour MP and on the Friday the blogger was interviewed by Radio 4 about his research. Within a week, the debate on MPs' expenses had gained a whole new dimension and the electoral reform campaign was propelled much higher up the political agenda.

So, the lesson for journalists here is that if you make friends with the people doing the research you may be able to come up with some interesting angles and get the story before your rivals. To do this I have four tips:

1   Don't abuse our goodwill and passion – e.g. unless agreed at the start, don't make us, in effect, do your job and write your story for you by doing all your research, answering streams of questions and being on call all hours. We have other work to do too (and sometimes a life); we are just so keen for our campaign to succeed we can forget that in order to give you the best story possible.

2   Do take us out for coffee occasionally to allow us to give you a more in-depth briefing on the bigger picture of our areas, or our thoughts on the big issues coming up. It makes us feel valued for more than our ability to give immediate short quotes; and also means we are more likely to think of you when we have some big juicy story we are looking to give as an exclusive, or simply want to pass on some interesting nugget.

3   Be clearer on deadlines and what you want when you want us to comment quickly on a story. With so much being online rather than in print, timings – and size of comment – can vary hugely and so it's good if we get a steer from you, so we can best respond.

4   If there's a particular route you prefer to receive press releases by (i.e. your own email address, via newsdesk, via editor) let us know and we will try and do that. We often don't have dedicated software or lists for sending out releases and have to rely on old or partial lists, cobbled together with our own more recent additions – so any help you can give us in ensuring our release goes to the right person is always much appreciated.

From the PR – Jayne Phenton

Jayne Phenton is Media Coordinator at Living Streets, a charity that stands up for pedestrians and works to create safe, attractive, enjoyable streets.

We're often surprised by what journalists choose to highlight in their stories. For Walk to School Week 2013 we issued a report, *Must Try Harder*, which was like a school report and it highlighted how the numbers of children walking to school were continuing to decline (currently at 46 per cent), and the failure of the government to take any significant measures to tackle the issue of active school travel.

We thought that the health issue would be the attention grabber, but three major newspapers went with the 'parents fear speeding cars' angle. We were pleased because it was all good coverage, but for people working in press offices the lesson is that you can't control what is written. For journalists, the lesson is that you often get good stories by trying to think of different angles to those being presented to you, and to always read the full report and not just the press release, as it may give you other ideas.

Part II

You've got an idea, now what?

10 Finding a hook

At the beginning of this book we explored the formula for feature ideas:

> Feature idea = Subject + Angle + Audience

However, to maximise your chance of getting a commission, you should add another element to this – the hook (also sometimes called a 'peg'):

> Feature idea = (Subject + Angle + Audience) + Hook

That is, once you have your idea, you also need to find a reason for why it should be written, and published, now, instead of tomorrow or next month or next year (depending on the frequency of your publication).

Think of the word 'hook' as having two meanings here. The first is to hook, or peg, your article to a reason for having it published now, to make it current and relevant. The second is so that your reader, realising how 'now' your article is, is hooked and reeled in and cannot resist reading it.

Of course, sometimes it is the hook that first leads to an idea, be it a news story you have read or knowledge of an upcoming event. In these cases you start with the hook and then have to work out your angle and audience in order to flesh out your idea.

But often the rest of an idea comes first, and then you need to work out how to make it current in order to persuade an editor to commission it.

Do not despair though, as it is very easy to find a hook whatever your article. Look at it this way – editors are looking for a reason to say yes to your idea because they have many pages to fill, rather than an excuse to say no (they do not need an excuse, they can just ignore your pitch). So, your hook is a way of giving them that reason.

Let's use as an example an idea for an article about why school class sizes are so important when it comes to choosing a primary school for your child. The main audience for this piece would be parents of children due to start school in the next couple of years. And for the purposes of this example we won't worry about crafting an enthralling introduction (we cover that in the next chapter), but just focus on exploring how the hook might work. And please note I have made up facts here to illustrate the point, so please don't reproduce any as being true.

There are many types of hooks you could find for such a piece; some ideas are given below.

A diarised event

By diarised, we mean an event that you know is coming. i.e. it is in the diary, or news planner. For example, in the UK the school year begins in September and school application forms need to be completed by the preceding January.

• With three weeks left for parents to fill out application forms for their child's school place, we look at the importance of class size as a factor in that choice.

A non-diarised event

Unlike a diarised event, a non-diarised event is something that is unplanned, that you (and other journalists) do not know is going to happen in advance. To find this you need to be out in society, talking to your contacts or making new contacts. Perhaps, for example, you speak to some parents of children at a local school and find out that class sizes have recently expanded beyond recommended levels and they do not feel their children are receiving individualised attention. You then speak to the school and verify this information.

• It's not just because official guidelines tell schools to do it that class sizes are kept to a maximum size, but because when they go over this size children and parents feel that pupils are not given individualised attention, as parents at xxx school in xxx found out this week.

New research or a survey

If you have good contacts in a subject area they will probably alert you to new research coming up, or you could call them to ask what new things are happening in their field. Or sometimes you may hear about this via a press release from a university, think tank or PR agency.

• Research due to be released next week will look at the impact of class sizes on learning outcomes and suggest that this is a key factor that parents should consider when choosing a school for their child.

Someone famous says something

If someone famous says something relevant it can be used as a hook, whether they are famous in that field or not.

- [Famous person] said this week that they will be home educating their child because class sizes in schools are too large. Certainly class size is one of a number of factors that parents must consider when choosing a school for their child.

Someone famous does something

The famous person might not even pass comment on a subject, but if it is reported that they have done something, that can be your hook.

- [Famous person] was seen looking round schools in Hollywood this week. No doubt one of the things they will have been looking at is class size, one of the most important factors when it comes to choosing a school.

Someone famous could feasibly do something

The famous person and what they say or do is practically irrelevant if they could feasibly do something.

- As [famous person's] daughter reaches school age this year, they will be thinking about where she should go to school. One of the things they need to be thinking about will be class sizes.

A political announcement is made...

If any level of government says something will be done, this can constitute a hook.

- The Government has announced new maximum class sizes for primary schools in a bid to improve attainment for all children. This will certainly be on parents' minds as they consider options for their own children.

...Or when no announcement is forthcoming

- An expected announcement on class sizes from the Education Secretary didn't happen this week but nevertheless it is an issue that will be at the forefront of parents' minds as they make their choices for their children's education.

People are told they should do something

- 'The issue of class sizes needs to be addressed urgently', said a leading teachers' association spokesperson this week. This is something that should certainly be on parents' minds as they choose a school for their child.

An anniversary

An anniversary of any of the above could be used as a hook.

- It is five years since the government announced a maximum class size for all schools, and it's still an issue that parents should consider when choosing a school.
- Research ten years ago showed a marked link between class size and child attainment. A decade on, the link remains and cannot be ignored by parents considering their options for schools.
- It's seven weeks since a leading teachers' association said the issue of class sizes needs to be addressed and the subject has touched a nerve at the school gate where parents are comparing notes and exploring their options.

Trend

If you have heard of something unusual happening in more than one place perhaps it is a new trend that can be used as a hook.

- In a bid to ensure that each child gets the help they need, some schools around the country have been eschewing traditional classes and splitting their pupils up into small groups made up of children across the year groups. Opinion on this varies, but teachers are enthusiastic, and think parents should also be keen.

Case study

Or if you can't find enough examples to be a trend, but you do have one strong example, this can also be a hook.

- At X school in X, pupils spend most of the day in groups of ten, leading their own learning and only calling for their teacher when they get stuck. It's not conventional, but the results are breathtaking. As parents consider options for their children, class sizes will be high on their agenda.

Something is happening somewhere else

You can localise a story that is happening elsewhere, using that as a hook and making it relevant to your own readers.

- Over 3,000 miles away from the Department of Education on Whitehall, 90 children sit in a small room in Kabul listening to their teacher. Such a scene would be unimaginable in the UK, where maximum class sizes have been in place for several years. Yet literacy levels are comparable. So do parents set too much store by class sizes rather than teaching?

These examples of hooks can work for most subjects, whether serious or more lifestyle based. Take, for example, the above types of hook, and an article looking at which kind of skirt suits which body shape. Again, I have made up facts to illustrate the point so don't reproduce any of these as actual facts.

A diarised event

- London Fashion Week starts next month and it's predicted to be the year of the skirt.

A non-diarised event

- Pop to your local high street and ask fashion store managers what item is selling best this week. I did just that and they unanimously told me skirts are flying off the shelves – long ones, short ones, flared ones, straight ones, it's all about the skirt.

New research or a survey

- The average woman has six skirts in her wardrobe, found a survey carried out by fashion brand X this week.

Someone famous says something

- 'I never wear trousers' said [famous person] last month. 'I prefer skirts. They are far more comfortable.'

Someone famous does something

- [Famous person] was seen wearing a bright yellow puffball skirt yesterday, a style not seen in public since 1985. So is it time to raid your mum's wardrobe and start searching vintage shops for a copy?

Someone famous could feasibly do something

- [Famous person] was seen shopping this week. With the summer coming up she may well have been looking for a new skirt.

A political announcement (or non-announcement)

- An expected rise in VAT is likely to make your shopping sprees more expensive from next month, so now is the time to stock up on some staples for your wardrobe.

An anniversary

- It is ten years since [famous person] wore 'that skirt', and still we are all talking about it.

Trend

- I was at a bar last night and looked around at the clientele. All the women, and some of the men, were wearing skirts. There wasn't a pair of jeans or chinos in sight. Clearly, this is the year of the skirt.

Case study

- X only owns two skirts. But she never wears trousers. Buy your skirts carefully, she says, and you can dress them up or down for any occasion.

Something is happening somewhere else

- Something is happening in New York City and that something is swishy. The skirt is back and you see it everywhere, from hipsters in Williamsburg to high maintenance princesses strolling through Central Park. It's a look that we in the UK could learn from.

My story: Lucy Jolin

Lucy Jolin is a freelance journalist and lecturer in journalism.

If you are using something as a hook, always discard the first idea you have. It will be too obvious and boring and everyone else will already have thought of it.

Anniversaries are, in fact, really good, though you may be put off by the idea of every other person in the world writing about the same one. The trick to this is to come up with a weird anniversary that nobody has yet thought of.

Never use an anniversary that you already know about. My best one was using the fiftieth anniversary of Philip Larkin's poem *Annus Mirabilis* that talks about how sex began in 1963, as a hook for a feature on teen fandom. I was absolutely delighted when a friend came up with the same idea two months later and I had been the first.

I've also used the thousand-year anniversary of an obscure mediaeval manuscript for a feature on the history of medical textbooks. I quite like having the idea of what I want to write about first and then going and hunting for an anniversary to hook it to, which is probably the wrong way round, but it seems to work.

Very occasionally, if a story is strong enough, you can get away without a hook. But it is rare for a feature to be so absolutely fascinating that you can convince an editor to go for this.

Of course, hooks don't always need to be in the introduction to an article. It may be that it is better woven in a little further down, or perhaps it will be clear from the headline or strapline, or even from the pictures used.

But before your idea is ready, you need to be sure of two things:

1   what your hook is
2   that your hook works with the timescale of the publication.

In terms of timescale of publication, what is meant is that the hook seems current. For a daily newspaper that may mean your hook has to be happening on the day of publication, or certainly as close to this as possible. For a bi-monthly publication you would have more leeway.

If I am stuck for ideas I often find it handy to start making a list of some upcoming hooks. Depending on the type of publication I am wanting to write for, this might be a week away (if pitching to a daily newspaper) or several months away (for a monthly magazine). More sensibly, rather than wait for a lull in ideas to start making your list, it is wise to keep a list of hooks as and when you come across them and think of them. This can stretch several years in advance.

For example, like many in Britain I have been watching *Strictly Come Dancing* on television, and at the time of writing this book it is hosted by two women instead of the more usual one man and one woman team. When the next series is about to begin I might want to write a piece looking at how this has been received by the public, or whether there has been a growth in prime time female-only presenting pairs.

Also, while writing this book singer Meghan Trainor became the first act to enter the UK top 40 based purely on streams of her music. It would be good to follow this up in six months or a year to see if others do this, or to look back at her career in a year's time, or to revisit the topic once there have been a certain number of songs that have done this – perhaps when 40 songs have made the Top 40 in this way.

Also, a news story on the BBC while writing this book said: 'Everyone in England will have access to GP services seven days a week by 2020, Prime Minister David Cameron has promised.' It would be worth revisiting this three years before the deadline, or one year before, and worth contacting the Department of Health to find out when the actual deadline will be in 2020.

Tip: Wait for your hook

Dina Rickman has worked as a freelance journalist and is now deputy news editor for the *i100* website of the *Independent*.

I wrote an article for the *Telegraph* about programmes in the UK that help abusive men reform. The headline was 'Violence against women: I punched my wife in the face. Now I'm trying to change'. It came from going to a Parliamentary event about people who work with domestic violence perpetrators, which I found out about via Twitter. I waited until there was a domestic violence story in the news so I had a hook, which was an EU study that showed a third of women have been physically or sexually assaulted.

Having a 'hooks diary' that stretches several years ahead can be very useful. When something interesting happens, put it in your hooks diary, so when you have a quiet period coming up and you know you need some ideas, you can have a look a little way ahead and see what things are coming up that you may be able to write about.

Things you might like to list in your diary include:

- anniversaries of events
- when something new has happened
- Government promises
- when famous people will be a certain age.

And you might categorise your entries according to the specific dates, anniversaries, years or even seasons.

You might also like to jot down ideas next to the entries as and when they occur to you. And don't worry if you can't use the idea this time round – you might be too busy when the fifth anniversary comes up, but bear it in mind for the tenth anniversary. Feature writing is a long-term career and your diary is a long-term investment.

Examples of entries might include those listed below.

2016

Hook – 20 years since the Orange Prize (for fiction by women) was launched (now called Bailey's prize). Long list in March. shortlist and winner in June.

- Has this prize changed things for women writers?
- Do literary prizes matter?

30 June 2017

Hook – 20 years since the first Harry Potter was published.

- A history of witches and wizards in children's books.
- Harry Potter was famously written in a coffee shop. Where do aspiring writers go to work these days?

3rd November

Hook – On this day in 1957, Russians launched a dog into space.

- Famous explorer animals.

2020

Hook – All the major political parties in the UK signed up to a pledge in 1999 to end Child Poverty in the UK by 2020.

- How is poverty measured and how has this changed over the years?
- What is life like for children living in poverty?
- Breaking the cycle – how have adults who grew up in poverty broken the cycle?
- What do politicians who were instrumental in establishing the pledge think needs to be done now?

Autumn

Hook – in Autumn 2014 ankle socks were all over the catwalk.

- How to make socks look cool.
- People show off their novelty socks.
- The life of a sock designer.

Tip: Sign up

It can be useful to sign up to as many newsletters, press release lists and press alerts as possible so that you have a steady stream of hooks in your inbox. It is easy to become overwhelmed by these, however, and well worth setting up a separate email account just for these, and then you can look through them during quiet periods.

My story – Jude Rogers

Jude Rogers is a freelance feature writer and lectures in journalism at London Metropolitan University.

Every year newspapers always want Christmas features. They always have round-ups and a review of the year but they also want other features that will get people reading them and get hits on the website. Coming up with ideas for that can be quite hard because it happens every year and everyone's already read about the stories behind the Christmas songs or people listing their favourite Christmas songs.

One year I thought what if I actually went and wrote a Christmas song myself and wrote a feature about it. There's always someone releasing a Christmas song and keen to plug it. So I found a singer-songwriter called Teddy Thompson who is pretty well known in the folk world. He was releasing a Christmas single and I knew he wasn't so famous that he wouldn't be interested. I thought he was the kind of artist who might not get a lot of publicity in the mainstream press because he's popular in folk circles but not really known in mainstream circles. So I suggested this to my editor who liked the

(Continued)

(Continued)

idea of me embarrassing myself, and Teddy Thompson's publicist was really into the idea too.

I went to his mum's flat in Earl's Court in London with my mum's guitar. I was wearing green and I began the piece talking about how I looked like a Christmas tree. It was a nice way to talk to somebody about how you go about writing a new sort of Christmas song, but also gave me a great springboard to talk about Christmas songs in general. In the end we wrote a song called *I'm going to kill you this Christmas*. It was very tongue in cheek. I thought the *Guardian* would like it because they could put an audio element in it on the website too. We spoke a lot about what makes a song – verses and chorus, instrumentation, good themes, etc., and it was published in the Christmas edition of the music section.

The following year I wrote another Christmas feature. I thought, wouldn't it be good to get a panel of Christmas experts from different fields to judge from that year's batch of Christmas singles and say which was the most Christmassy. You have to use your contacts book creatively. Giles Fraser, who had just left St Paul's Cathedral and was in the news, had been my college chaplain at university. I knew that he's quite fun and would like the idea and could talk about the Christian side of Christmas and how that was expressed in these songs. My brother was doing a degree in music at Bristol University so I got one of his tutors who was an expert in medieval music and traditional Christmas music and also a woman, which was great because I didn't want an all-male panel. On an industry message board I managed to find someone who is a Christmas party planner, so they did it because they were able to plug their company. The final one was Mike Batt. He wrote *A Winter's Tale*, sung by David Essex and The Wombles' Christmas song, and that year The Wombles were coming back with another Christmas song, and I had interviewed him earlier in the year for something else so knew him and his publicist already.

What I did was get some Christmas songs – classics, novelty songs and new releases, and sent links to the songs to each judge. They had to listen to them, rate them out of ten for different Christmas elements and then I rang them up to interview them about their answers. It was a nice mix of a religious approach, a musical approach and a party approach.

Remember, sometimes you can start with a hook, and use that as an inspiration for your feature idea. Other times you start with a subject and then search for a hook. Either way is fine.

And, of course, there is another way, as a feature writer, to find a hook, which is to make yourself the hook. It doesn't work for all features, but sometimes you can get away with it. For example, a feature about making great cakes at home might begin something like this:

> I ate a delicious slice of cake the other day, the type that you will remember in ten years' time while sitting in a boring meeting at work and before you know it you'll be drooling and sighing and sniffing the air for strawberry jam and vanilla while Mike from Accounts talks deficits and bottom lines. Here's how to replicate it at home...

Task: Identify hooks

Take any newspaper or magazine (or, if you do not have one to hand, use www.bbc.co.uk/news/magazine) and look at the features. Work out what the hook is for each. Sometimes there is more than one.

Article title	Hook 1	Hook 2 (if there is one)

Task: Find multiple hooks

Think of a subject you would like to write about (no need for an angle or audience at this stage). Find as many hooks as you can using the categories we've looked at above. Be creative.

Subject:	
Type of hook	*Possible hook*
A diarised event	
A non-diarised event	
New research or a survey	
Someone famous has said something	
Someone famous has done something	
Someone famous could feasibly do something	
A political announcement (or non-announcement)	
People are being told they should do (or not do) something	
An anniversary	
Trend	
Case study	
Something is happening somewhere else	

Task: Start with the hook

Find a good hook (perhaps go to an 'On this day' website and see what happened this day several years ago). Starting with the hook, try to come up with as many feature ideas as you can.

Tip: Quotes as hooks

Have a good Dictionary of Quotations to hand. You can search for quotes by subject area and they can often give you a good hook, such as the anniversary of a famous speech or poem or even the birth or death of the person who made the speech or wrote the poem.

For example, I looked up quotes about fish and found that, in 1951, Herbert Hoover, who was President of the United States from 1929–33, said in a speech in Florida that 'all men are equal before fish'.

What a lovely hook this could potentially be – if I write a feature in 2021 about cooking fish I may well begin it: 'Seventy years ago Herbert Hoover said "all men are equal before fish" but, as any regular cook of seafood knows, all fish are not equal before man.' Or something like that.

11 Key components of your article

As we explored at the beginning of this book, there are many types of feature article including, no doubt, types that you will invent yourself in due course when you realise that what you have just written doesn't fall into any existing category.

Excluding basic list type features, or features wholly based on case studies, most features will include at least some of the following components. As a feature writer, you can include or exclude these as you see fit, but it is wise to familiarise yourself with the list so you are doing so as a deliberate act of inclusion or omission rather than as an oversight.

(In no particular order other than the introduction and conclusion):

- Introduction
- Hook
- Case studies
- Quotes – from experts (including opposing ones), from case studies and from other people who have reason to have an opinion on or insight into the subject
- Both sides of the argument
- Statistics and facts
- Description/colour
- Background information
- The relevance for the reader
- A call to action/a moral lesson
- Conclusion.

Let's take each of these in turn:

Introduction

Forget everything you have ever learned in news writing or academic writing. A feature introduction doesn't necessarily answer the who, what, where, why, when and how of a story. Nor does it necessarily even tell you what the feature will be about or where you will go with it. In feature writing the purpose of the introduction is to make you want to read the next paragraph. In fact, that is one of the jobs of every paragraph (or sentence, or maybe even every word) in a feature – to make you move on to the next one rather than stop reading. A successful feature is one where the reader has read right to the end. And, unlike an academic essay, where you are told to tell the reader what you are going to tell them, tell it to them, then tell them what you told them, a feature takes its readers by surprise, leading them through twists and turns so that reading it is an adventure. You do not necessarily want your readers to know from the introduction what they will be thinking by the conclusion.

Often a good introduction plonks the reader right in the middle of a story. Certainly, purely chronological features are often the least exciting to read. Here's an example of a potential introduction for a feature about the 2004 tsunami in the Indian Ocean:

> There were no queues outside the hospitals in Phuket the day after the 2004 tsunami hit. In fact, there were no hospitals. They had all been washed away. 'We set up camp on what seemed to be a marsh though it had, the week before, been a main road', said John Smith, an aid worker who flew to the scene the day after.

This is far more effective than:

> In 2004 a huge tsunami in the Indian Ocean changed the way our generation would view the sea forever.

It's not a bad sentence, but perhaps would be better later in the piece.

If you are struggling, however, there are six fallback introduction types you can rely on to help you. Here are some examples based on a feature idea about the impact of school class sizes on pupils' achievement (with descriptions and facts made up by me for the purposes of this example).

1   *Set the scene/paint a picture*   It's a typical classroom. The windows look out onto an empty playground. There is a faint smell of school dinner cabbage in the air. Bunsen burners are set out on the front table. There should be one for each student but because of class sizes they are shared between three, sometimes four, students. This lack of equipment is not just irritating for students, but could severely damage their future life chances, as new research shows secondary school class sizes have a huge impact on exam results. (This doesn't have to be a true scene, as long as it is roughly accurate.)

2   *Start with a quote*   'I like school,' says Joe Bloggs, a twelve-year-old from Luton, 'but I don't like having to shout to be heard.' For Joe Bloggs, however, in a class of 35 students, unless he shouts the teacher won't even realise he is there. Class sizes in schools such as Joe's are

having a huge effect on children's potential future achievement, new research shows.

3   *Statistics*   95 per cent of secondary school students are in classes of over 30 pupils, shows new research out this month. As exam season looms, we look at what this means for their achievements and future career prospects.

4   *Put into context*   As politicians continue to harp on about primary school class sizes, they are failing to mention the most important issue facing children today – secondary school class sizes. A new report out this month seeks to examine what big classes mean in terms of actual achievement, and its conclusions are shocking.

5   *Use your hook*   As the nation's schoolchildren head back to the classroom this week, new research has been published that says it's not what they learn but how many are there when they learn it that matters.

6   *Start with the counterargument*   Some people claim that if all children were quiet and listened to their teacher then there could be 200 kids in the room and it wouldn't matter. But new research published this week shows this is just not true.

Hook

We looked at hooks in detail in the previous chapter. The hook is what makes your article relevant now, and the reason why it should be published in the current issue rather than any other. You'll need a hook to convince your editor to publish your piece. Except, of course, when you don't – occasionally a story is strong enough to make it through to publication without a hook, but these times are rare.

Case studies

A case study is a real life example of someone who has done what you are writing about, or should have done it, or wishes they had, or knew someone who did it once. Basically, it adds human colour to the piece and makes it real. If you are writing about how to have a friendly divorce, for example, then you would need comments about the experiences of people who have done this in real life, and perhaps from those who failed to do it too.

So, an article about the health risks in refugee camps would talk to refugees living in the camp and health workers on the ground. An article about curly hair styles would talk to people with curly hair, and an article about people who have had to sell their possessions in order to pay for their child's school trip would talk to people who had actually done this.

You may start with a case study as inspiration for your idea – someone tells you an interesting story about their life, for example. An example of this is when I wrote an article about how schools can often fail to keep in touch with both parents of their pupils when the parents are no longer a couple. This came from the husband of a friend complaining in conversation how his children's schools sent all letters to his ex-wife and none to him, despite him having joint custody of the children.

Or you may have an idea and then look for case studies – such as wanting to write a feature about people who have changed career in their fifties and then setting out to find them.

There are many ways to find case studies. Some favourites are:

- Go to relevant charities; they may have people they work with who fit the bill.
- Look on relevant forums.
- Find people who have been in articles before and contact them again (though make sure your publication knows that they have appeared in the press before).
- Ask journalists who have written about the subject before to share their contacts with you (as long as you are prepared to repay the favour one day).
- Ask everyone you know, each of whom will know other people.
- Specifically, ask PRs you know as they may have someone who fits the bill who will talk about what you need in return for a plug for their company, product or cause.
- Use social media (but remember once it's out there other people will know what ideas you are currently working on).
- Go to where the people will be (e.g. if want to talk to a stripper, then go to a strip club).

Quotes

Most features need quotes. These are usually from case studies (as detailed above), experts (including those with opposing views) and from other people who have reason to have an opinion on or insight into the subject.

By doing the research required to write your article, you are now an expert on it. However, you need to show the reader that you haven't plucked this knowledge from thin air, but that you have gone to real experts in the field for their opinion and knowledge.

Inexperienced feature writers often worry about finding experts. Often the problem is that they find an expert and fixate on speaking to them, and are then disappointed when that expert is on a year-long holiday with no means of communication, not interested in talking to them, not an expert in that area after all or quite simply busy.

But for most subjects it should not be hard to find experts to talk about what you are covering in your article. It shouldn't even be hard to find friendly articulate experts who want to talk to you. In fact, for nearly everything you should be able to compile quite a long list of appropriate experts, and work your way through them until you have all the information, opposing viewpoints and other information that you need.

Experts include:

- *Academics*   These may be the people who have carried out specific research in the field you are writing about, or people in their team or their students, or their bosses, or other academics who disagree with them or those in the same field who can give you an overview of the work being done. Universities often have directories of experts on their websites listing the expertise of their staff.
- *Charities, trade unions, think tanks, pressure groups and support groups*   Nearly every subject will have at least one such organisation, and usually many, who can comment on goings on in that field.
- *Elected representatives and official bodies*   Depending on the subject and the geographical area that your feature is about you may be able to find an appropriate councillor, mayor, member of parliament or other elected representative to comment for you. You may also find that going through official channels, such as civil service press offices or local government press offices, yields some results. As you build up your contacts you can usually circumvent these channels and go straight to the relevant person.
- *Other journalists*   Journalists who have written about this subject before may well be experts on it in their own right and may be able to help you, either by commenting in their own right or by briefing you on the issues or passing on contacts.
- *Other interested parties*   Depending on what you are writing about you may well find people who are experts because they have experienced something similar. If you are writing an article about banning dangerous dogs, for example, you may find a dog owner on your street who will talk, or their neighbour, or a pet shop, or a breeder.
- *Social media*   There is a growing trend for publications to take tweets (from Twitter) or comments from other social media and use these as expert comments or barometers of the public mood in articles. I think this is often lazy journalism, unless your article is about social media or unless the person you are quoting is an expert you would want to talk to anyway.

Let's take as an example a story that is in the news at the time of writing this book – the crash of the Virgin Galactic SpaceShipTwo in October 2014. Two pilots were on SpaceShipTwo at the time of the accident, one of whom died and one of whom used their ejector button and parachuted clear.

Let's imagine you had been commissioned to write a feature for the pages of a national newspaper, looking at how people react when there is a life or death crisis and a couple of seconds to decide whether to press a button to escape.

If I were writing this feature I would start by making a list of the things I would want people to talk to me about. In this case:

- What it is like to be in that situation (i.e. people who have done this and survived).
- People who can comment on those who didn't survive (i.e. people working at ground control when there have been fatal accidents).
- Someone to fill me in on the history of similar accidents – probably an author, blogger or academic.
- Someone who can talk about the psychology of split-second decision making.

I would then compile a list of people who might be able to do the above. To find them I would:

- Look at who has been quoted in news stories about this.
- Read previous features written about this subject and similar subjects to see who was quoted.
- Search for universities that specialise in the study of exploration or accidents or aeronautical engineering to look for an expert to comment.
- Contact psychologists through their professional body to find an expert in this area.
- Find out who the bodies that investigate such accidents are and see whether they have anyone available for comment.
- Search for books and broadcasts on this issue and talk to their authors/ makers.
- Think about other related industries where similar incidents happen – in this case civil aviation and the military, and speak to experts in those fields by contacting relevant companies or departments and seeing if they can put you in touch with anyone.
- Search for blogs and forums about this subject.

Given that Virgin is a British company, and the accident happened in the United States, I would feel able to use experts from either side of the Atlantic, branching out to experts from other countries if I wasn't able to get hold of these.

Of course, depending on what the people I talk to say, my article may go in an unexpected direction, or I may have further questions that I need to ask of different experts.

And, of course, you should never forget to end your chats with the key question: 'Is there anyone else you think I should talk to about this?' You should ask this of people who are able to help you, and people who say they are unable to help you – it never hurts to have more experts you can call if necessary, if not for now then for future pieces.

Task: Find multiple experts

Using internet research to follow the approach outlined above, or any other approach you can think of, try to come up with the names and contact details for 20 relevant experts.

This may seem like a lot but it means that the pressure is taken off if you can't get hold of an expert, or if they don't have anything helpful to say or they communicate badly, or just don't want to talk to you. In fact, I would often have double this number of experts in mind before beginning my research, so that I would be confident that I would get hold of at least some people who could help me.

Name	Job title	Contact number	Email/Twitter handle/other contacts	Notes (e.g. time zone they are in)
1				
2				
3				
4				
5				
6				
7				
8				
9				
10				
11				
12				
13				
14				
15				
16				
17				
18				
19				
20				

As for finding people to quote who may have a reason to be quoted – try thinking about who else may have an opinion on this. In the case of the above example I would be keen to get comments from people who witnessed the accident, people who were related to people who had been in similar accidents, people with tickets for space flights with the company and maybe even normal people who dream of going to space one day.

Task: List the experts

Look at any feature from any publication. Make a list of the experts quoted. In what way are they an expert (e.g. personal experience, through work)? Do this for several features and you will build up a list of the types of people you can go to for expert opinion.

Tip: Have some stock questions

Have a list of helpful questions to ask all experts, in addition to specific questions about the subject you are writing about. It may include things like:

- Can you explain any jargon you may have used – what words would my readers be unlikely to understand?
- How does whatever we are talking about affect everyday life?
- What should I have asked you that I didn't?
- Who else do you recommend I talk to?
- Are there any interesting issues or developments coming up in your field that I should keep an eye on? (Good for future feature ideas.)
- Are there any big anniversaries or events coming up in your field? (Good for your list of hooks.)

Tip: Language you can understand

Don't be afraid to ask people to explain what they have said in language that your readers (and you) can easily understand.

And, if something doesn't make sense when you are reading back your notes, call them again to clarify. They will prefer that to being misquoted.

Both sides of the argument

If there is an argument or theory being expounded, either in the article as a whole or by someone being quoted in the article, then you should at least acknowledge any opposing view.

Statistics and facts

There are three types of journalist, goes the joke that can be adapted to absolutely any group of people. Those who can add up, and those who can't.

Even when you don't at first realise it, nearly all features are jam-packed with facts and statistics. Not only do these legitimise the article, giving it a sense of authority, but they fulfil the role we spoke about at the beginning of this book, of making sure that the reader, upon finishing an article, becomes an expert in the subject being covered, even if it is in a very narrow area.

One of my favourite ever features was published in the *Observer* in 1997 and was written by Kathryn Flett. It was a travel feature, about romantic weekends in the Belgian city of Bruges, but instead of being a romantic trip she had just been told by her husband that he was leaving her. Upon first reading, the article is about the emotions involved in a break-up. We hear about the tears (hers) and the quiet resolve and stoicism (his), the false politeness and the lack of eye contact and conversation. If you were asked after reading it you would probably say that the feature was about a relationship not about Bruges.

And yet woven into the tale of relationship woe are loads of facts about Bruges:

- That it took three hours and 25 minutes to get the train from London to Brussels.
- That you catch the connecting train to Bruges from Brussels Midi station and it takes 50 minutes.
- The hotel they stayed at, Die Swaene, is a ten-minute cab ride from Bruges station.
- Die Swaene is three old townhouses of four stories and has 'a curtained reception area and a creaky elevator'.
- At the time of writing (some years ago now) the 'Romeo and Juliet' weekend cost $337.
- At Die Swaene room service is available.
- In the 1300s, 150 ships moored in Bruges every day, though the estuary is now silted up.
- Bruges has eight miles of canal.
- One of its churches is the twelfth-century Basilica of the Holy Blood, and it claims to own a clot of Jesus's blood.

- Fries, mussels and beer are typical fare in Bruges.
- Simon Stevinplein is a small square named after the man who introduced the decimal system to Bruges and invented dikes.

In other words, you are given all the facts you would expect to read in a travel feature, relationship break up or not.

Nearly all features weave such facts into their writing. The best do it without the reader even noticing it is being done, except that by the end of the feature you appear to miraculously know new things.

When writing your feature you should think of it as the Pub Quiz Effect (for non-British or Irish readers, pub quizzes are a cultural phenomenon in the UK and Ireland, in which teams go to pubs or bars and complete against each other in general knowledge quizzes).

Ask yourself, does your feature give you answers to questions that could potentially come up in a pub quiz, albeit in an obscure round? For example, after reading Kathryn Flett's piece you would know the answer to 'Which basilica in Bruges claims to own a clot of Jesus's blood?'. If your article has no such facts, it probably needs some.

This is the case even for a how to or list article. Imagine you are writing a simple how to feature on how to change a fuse and plug – perhaps it is for a publication aimed at people who have just moved to the UK and are not familiar with the way the electrics work. If the article is written comprehensively your reader, upon finishing it, would be able to answer the following pub quiz style questions:

- In a standard UK plug, what colour is the live wire?
- You can use a three amp fuse for appliances up to how many watts?

Task: Find the facts

Choose any feature from any publication. Make a list of every fact or statistic you can find in it. For example, an article about toast may include facts such as 'every minute 10,000 loaves of bread are sold in Britain' and 'most bread sold in the UK is made in Derbyshire' and 'jam is Britons' favourite toast topping' and 'bread originated as a food in North Africa' and 'Sainsbury's sells 40 different varieties of bread', etc. (I have made all of these up – please do not repeat them as truth!)

Description/colour

The point of descriptive writing, often called colour, is to make the reader feel as if they were actually there with you. So, if you are interviewing someone who sprays themselves with perfume every five minutes, you would want to include this. If the lobby of a government department goes quiet every time the lift doors open, write that. It's far more effective to do so than to tell us that your interviewee is worried about their smell or that the atmosphere in a department is one of expectation and anxiety in case a key person appears. You've probably heard this before as 'show, don't tell'.

Basically, you need to make your reader feel as if they have been wherever it is you are describing, so that if they were kidnapped and dumped somewhere random that happened to have been the focus of your feature then they should recognise it from having read your article, be it the Gobi Desert or an Accident and Emergency Department or a particular fashion store.

When writing a description it is hard to strike a balance between being purely functional ('the walls were grey, the seats were hard, the 30-year-old woman with blonde hair walked over and shook my hand') and being too flowery ('the air was rich with frangipani and the heady scent made me lightheaded as the blonde woman strode across the room like a rugby player and firmly grasped my hand').

What you need to bear in mind is the purpose for which you are using description. Sometimes it is to give the reader a sense of being there, so if you are writing about the desert you would want to mention the heat and the dust and the colours and the immaculate white dress of the person you are meeting as it helps the reader visualize, and feel, what you are talking about.

If you are using description to convey your opinion of a place or person, then you will be using language to subtly make your reader think what you want them to think.

Take, for example, the following two descriptions:

> The psychic was sitting at a small card table with a folded up playing card under one corner to stop it wobbling. Her earrings jangled as she opened her mouth and said quietly, so the heavies at the door couldn't hear, 'It's 50 quid for half an hour'.

> Her bodyguards flanked the doorway as I was shown in and she sat, a small figure at a small table, in the far corner of the dimly lit room. Her jewellery caught the light as she told me the terms of our meeting in a sexy whisper.

These could be descriptions of the same encounter but by choosing what to highlight and how you have interpreted certain things, very different impressions are given even though both are truthful (or not truthful in this case as I have made them up for illustrative purposes).

When you are making notes for a descriptive part of a feature, always do so at the time or as close to the time as possible – small details are rarely remembered as vividly after the event. You might find it helpful to ask yourself the following questions:

- What are they wearing? Is it old or new? Is it what you would expect someone to wear in this situation? Do they look 'right?' What are the colours? Where did they get it?
- How old do they look? Are they wearing make-up? What hair style and colour do they have? What do they smell like?
- Who else is around? What do they look like? Are they taking any notice of whatever you are reporting on?
- Take a picture of the scene in your head – if you were a detective what would be the clues that would lead you to deduce what was going on?
- Does the place smell? What furniture is there? Is there a predominant colour? What can you hear? Is there an atmosphere and what is it – fear, happiness, relaxation, excitement, etc?

Task: Go somewhere new

Go somewhere new – it could be a coffee shop or a road or a museum or a part of your garden you never usually stand in. Without thinking it through too much, write a description of it.

Next, think of the feeling you want to convey to your reader. Perhaps you want to make them think this place is incredibly exclusive, or that it has an air of terror. Without making anything up, pick out the details that can convey this feeling and write another description that does this.

Background information

This is the essential information the reader needs to know in order to understand the piece in context. Going back to the idea of a feature about how people react when there is a life or death crisis and a couple of seconds to decide whether to press a button to escape, with the Virgin Galactic SpaceShipTwo accident as a hook, your reader needs some information in order to properly understand the article. They need to know that Virgin is developing a commercial space flight programme, that it has suffered many delays to its schedule (and perhaps a history of this), including accidents such as this one. You may also want your readers to know about the founder of Virgin, Richard Branson, and his personal history as an explorer and businessman. Of course, the background information necessary varies depending on your audience – if you were writing for an aviation publication you might be able to assume that your readers know all of this.

You have to make similar judgement calls whatever the subject and audience. If your article includes a recipe, for example, and is written for a publication aimed at inexperienced home cooks, you may have to explain that 'season' means add salt and pepper. To do this in a publication for professional chefs may be considered patronising and unnecessary.

The relevance for the reader

Readers want to know how whatever they are reading about will impact on them, or if it doesn't, then at least why they should know about it. This may be covered by the hook, but may not be.

It may just be that the article is fascinating so makes the reader a better informed, more interesting person and that it aids their intellectual development.

Or it may be that the issues being discussed impact directly on their life.

Maybe the reader wants to be scared. Or wants to make themselves feel better. Perhaps they enjoy a mystery. Maybe they want to learn how to do something new or how to fit in, or just to feel ahead of the curve with knowledge of a new trend.

Or maybe they just want to pass the time.

The relevance to the reader – their reason for reading it – may be implicit or explicit, so in many ways this is a silent component. But think of a reader looking at the feature with you next to them, wondering aloud whether they should bother to read it. What reason would you give them to do so?

A call to action/a moral lesson

Often, though not always, an article will have a call to action. This may be a moral lesson or warning, or a note of optimism in some way or another. As a feature writer, you need to think, what do I want readers to do after reading this article? If you want them to go away and sign a petition, or buy a product, or implement a new skill you have taught them, or view the world in a new way, or stop doing something, or feel better about themselves, or read your next article on the same subject, or know how to stop something happening to them, and so on, then you need to be clear about the outcome expected and write your piece accordingly, even if this call to action is only implicit in your piece.

It may be that you just want readers to agree with you. Features do not tend to include overt references to the writer's opinion (though these conventions can always be broken, of course). This doesn't mean that the writer does not make their opinion clear, but they do it by pushing the reader towards that point of view using facts and argument and other people's opinions. So you are writing an article on sponge cakes and looking at whether they should be made with butter or margarine. If you strongly feel that butter is the right choice, you can say this. But it is much more effective to find an expert to say it for you and to quote them. So it's not that you don't put your opinion across, but you do so by choosing who to quote and which facts to highlight and which heartstrings to tug.

Conclusion

Of course, all features, even those that appear to be interminable, come to an end at some point. In a way, features don't have conclusions as such – they can end on anything providing there are no unanswered questions (unless that is the point of the feature). But feature writers frequently say that ending articles is hard. So, as with introductions, here are some ways to conclude a feature, using the same example I used with introductions of a piece looking at the link between class sizes and pupils' attainment, once again with all the information made up by me.

1   *A warning*   Unless schools tackle this issue then it doesn't matter how hard children work or how conscientious their teachers are, Britain will be unable to compete in the global marketplace.

2   *An optimistic note*   This groundbreaking work by one East London school could be the future. If schools around the country follow its lead we really will be the most progressive country in Europe.

3   *A practical suggestion*   Any changes in class sizes will cost money but, as the example from East London shows, it is well worth it. Perhaps the first step is to recruit more teachers so that in the future all children will get the individual attention they need.

4   *A quote*   This example from East London shows what can be done when the community pulls together to focus on its schools. 'I'm thrilled at our results despite the poor funding we receive,' says headteacher Josephine Bloggs. 'Imagine what could be achieved nationwide if everyone followed our example.'

12 Pitching and writing your article

You have your idea and you have your hook, now you just need a commission.

'Pitch' is the word used for the way you try to sell your idea to an editor.

Unless I have an incredibly timely idea that needs an urgent answer and is to an editor I know well, I always pitch by email.

There are two ways to pitch. The first is to spend a long time crafting your pitch, almost as if it is a mini article, spending time researching the facts and working out which experts you would quote and the likely conclusions your article will reach.

The second is to give just a quick flavour of the article idea and leave it for the editor to ask for more information if they want it.

I favour the second approach as freelancers do not get paid for preparatory work, only for actual work. If an editor likes the sound of your idea they can always ask for more information before they make a decision whether to commission the piece. But you should choose whichever approach works for you – the second way you have time to pitch more articles but probably get proportionately fewer commissions, the first way you pitch fewer pieces but more of those pitches may be successful.

Either way, the pitch has three essential components:

- who you are
- what the idea is
- the hook.

There are also some non-essential things you can include, such as whether you have a case study and whether they are prepared to be photographed, why you are the ideal person to write the piece and whether you have a time by which you need to know if the editor wants to commission it.

Here's an example:

Dear X,

I am a freelance journalist writing about food, trends and relationships for consumer magazines and newspapers.

Would you like an article for *Real Men* looking at the basic cake recipes your readers should be able to make this summer, especially if they want to impress potential partners by taking them on a homemade picnic? A survey out this month by an internet dating company found that people are five times more likely to have sex on a first date if the man has made a cake rather than bought it in a shop, yet only one in ten men know how to bake a Victoria Sponge.

I'd be ideal to write this piece as I met my own wife at a village fete by the cake stall while she was eating a brownie I had made. I also have a case study of a man who set up a cookery school for men and specialises in baking. He is happy to be photographed and is based in the north-east.

Please let me know as soon as possible as I would like to pitch this idea elsewhere if it is not for you.

Kind regards...

And here it is again with annotations:

Dear Dave, [Always try to find out the name of the person to pitch to. You can usually ring the editorial assistant to ask for the contact details.]

I am a freelance journalist writing about food, trends and relationships for consumer magazines and newspapers. [Here you can namedrop some publications you have written for if you wish.]

Would you like an article for *Real Men* looking at the basic cake recipes your readers should be able to make this summer, especially if they want to impress potential partners by taking them on a homemade picnic? A survey out this month by an internet dating company found that people are five times more likely to have sex on a first date if the man has made a cake rather than bought it in a shop, yet only one in ten men know how to bake a Victoria Sponge. [This paragraph combines the idea with the hook.]

I'd be ideal to write this piece as I met my own wife at a village fete by the cake stall while she was eating a brownie I had made. [There is no need to show why you are ideal – just being a journalist whose job it is to write should be enough. But if you have a reason you may as well include it.] I also have a case study of a man who set up a cookery school for men and specialises in baking. He is happy to be photographed and is based in the north-east. [Do not give away identifying details as this ensures the editor cannot just assign this story to another journalist – if they like the case study idea they now need you to write it as you have the case study details.]

Please let me know as soon as possible as I would like to pitch this idea elsewhere if it is not for you.

Kind regards…

Tip: Subject field

Use the subject field. Often that is all the recipient will have time to read.

There are two pieces of information that are very handy to know before sending out your pitch. The first is the name of the person you should pitch to – you should be able to get this by calling the editorial assistant or desk secretary and asking for it.

The second is the commissioning timetable of each issue. This will be different for every publication and will depend on how frequent the publication is. For a daily newspaper, for example, there may be early morning commissioning meetings, although weekly sections may be planned a long time in advance. On a monthly magazine they probably work three to four months ahead so there is no point pitching Christmas ideas in November. It is wise to either ask the editorial assistant whether there is a good time of day (for a daily paper) or day of the week (for a weekly publication) or time of month (for a monthly publication) to send your pitch. Get it right and it will arrive in the correct inbox at exactly the time that the commissioning editor is gathering their ideas together for the meeting where it will be decided what to commission.

Of course, it is not always possible to get these two pieces of information, but it is certainly worth trying.

Another thing to do before you phone to ask for this information is to work out a sentence that describes your pitch. This is in case the relevant editor picks up the phone and asks you to tell them, there and then, what your pitch is. In the movie business it's known as the 'elevator pitch' – how you would pitch your idea for a film to Steven Spielberg if you were in a lift with him for two minutes.

If you are struggling to work out your one sentence pitch then try to think how you would explain your idea to your nice but slightly dim mate over a coffee. Can't do it? Then your idea is too complicated. Even deeply intellectual questions and complicated analyses of world events can be distilled into a sentence – 'My feature looks at why people believe in God' or 'My feature explores the reasons for war in the Middle East and whether there is any possibility there could be peace' or 'It looks at achieving the perfect balance in a three-course meal so you feel full up but not overstuffed'.

People often ask whether it is okay to pitch the same idea to more than one publication at once. Everyone has a different answer to this but I think it is bad form to pitch the same idea to competitors without at least giving the first publication the chance to look at it and get back to you. If your idea is time sensitive you can always say in your pitch that you need to know that day, or that you will follow up with a phone call in an hour or so as you want to pitch it elsewhere if they don't want it.

You can pitch similar articles to publications that are not competing with each other but you should change your article slightly (which you would do anyway to suit each audience). You should also use different quotes and examples and, if a case study has already appeared in one publication, you should let your editor at the second publication know this.

The only exception I know of is case study based stories for real life magazines, where the convention seems to be to pitch your piece to as many places as possible and sell it to the highest bidder.

It is worth keeping a list of where you have pitched each idea so that you don't send the same idea to the same place more than once. As you should have several ideas at once and several pitches being considered by editors this is well worth doing properly so you can keep track of things. A simple table like this one would do the job perfectly:

Idea	One line pitch	1st pitch	2nd pitch	3rd pitch
Example How enthusiastic amateurs can make the perfect sponge cake at home	'This feature uses the recent surge in interest in home baking following The Great British Bake-off to show your readers how they can make a perfect sponge cake at home without any prior experience of baking and using just five ingredients.'	*Guardian* food pages Pitch sent 13/7/13 to Jane Smith [include contact details here]	*Indy* food pages	*Daily Express* food pages

Bingo! An editor liked your pitch and now you've got to write the piece. You know the typical components of a feature and you know how to do your research and find your case studies and experts. But what else do you need to know before you start writing?

Some editors, particularly on newspapers, leave it at this. You write the article yourself with little or no guidance and they don't have ay input until it is submitted.

Others, particularly those on glossy magazines, may issue you with a commissioning form more or less planning your article, and what it should include, for you.

Others may just give you a slight steer, asking you to use a particular expert or mention something specific.

Whatever their approach, there is some information you must make sure you get before you begin your piece:

- How long the article should be.
- The style of the article.
- Whether all names need to be real.
- Whether all case studies need to be photographed.
- How links and websites should be used.
- The deadline.
- How much you'll be paid (and when).

Although it can be daunting to ask these questions, and people often shy away from discussing money in particular, it actually marks you out as someone who knows what they are doing rather than the opposite. After all, if you are doing this for money, then it is a job, not a hobby. As I hope I have shown throughout this book, it is an enjoyable and privileged job, but it is still a job. Not only that, but it saves confusion later on if you get clarity on what is expected from you, and what you expect in return.

One of the most important lessons I have learned from editors during my time freelancing, is that they do not like to be taken by surprise and find out at the last minute that an article isn't going to be ready on time or that it has gone off at an unexpected angle. Once you know this is the case, and once you have a solution in mind (e.g. 'I can't meet your deadline with this piece but I can with another' or 'I couldn't make the original angle stand up but would you like this one instead?') then immediately let the editor know. They may be able to help you, and you telling them in good time allows them to find an alternative article to fill the slot, if necessary.

I have found that most editors will forgive things changing and work with you again (as long as it doesn't happen all the time), but they will not forgive being left at the last moment with a gaping hole in their publication that needs to be filled.

As with all careers, it is not necessarily those who are best who become successful. The successful ones are those who are competent, rather than geniuses, as long as the competence goes hand in hand with reliability – doing what you said you would when you said you would do it. That is, there is no point producing 1,000 words next week if the editor wanted 500 words this week.

Appendix: Ideas!

This book is mainly about finding ideas for features. Whether you are a commissioning editor of many years' experience, a freelancer wanting to find ways of coming up with new ideas, a blogger looking for inspiration for regular posts, or any other kind of writer, you have hopefully been shown some new ways to generate ideas.

There are four *very important things* to remember from this book:

1   If you think it is interesting, it probably is.
2   A feature idea needs a subject, an angle and an audience. Otherwise it is not a feature idea, just a partial one.
3   A feature makes the reader an expert in a very small area of a particular subject, and usually attempts to answer a question, though the question is not always made explicit.
4   You need to have the confidence to express your bad ideas, to yourself at least, in order to find your good ideas.

Task: Use the ideas from this book

Apply the lessons of this book – there are several hundred ideas in this book. Even if only one in ten of them is workable, that's still a lot of ideas. Go on, steal them. Make them your own. Remember, each one will be different depending on the angle your research leads to and your audience and the hook and the time you write it. So, even if hundreds of readers choose the same idea to develop, that should lead to hundreds of different features.

Uncomfortable doing that? Then come up with your own ideas. Here are 100 prompts for you, in the form of questions that you could ask yourself or others. Thinking about them should lead to lots of ideas. For example, question 75 asks what your partner doesn't know about you. Perhaps you have lied about how much money you spent on something – this could become an interesting feature on what happens when you (or someone else – these do not only have to spark personal feature ideas) tell your partner something they might not want to hear, or how to keep secrets, or signs that your relationship is in trouble. Or question 34 asks about the most exciting thing you have ever received through the post? If the answer to this is 'a letter from Santa' then perhaps you would be inspired to write a feature about the letter from Santa industry and who writes them all. And question 90, on whether you know the words to your national anthem, may make you think about writing a feature on how best to learn song lyrics, or how singers remember their songs, or actors remember their lines.

1 Which famous entrepreneurs can you name? What do they do? What else do you know about them?

2 How much money do you earn? Where do you think this comes in comparison to the national average? Look it up – were you right?

3 If you have children, what would you have done differently when they were babies, now that you know what you know?

4 What did you have for breakfast? Analyse why. Was it for convenience? For a health reason? Because you always have that?

5 What date is it today? What happened on this day at any time in the past? (There are many internet resources to help you find this out.)

6 What were you doing this time last year? This time five years ago? This time ten years ago? And so on.

7 If you could give your younger self any advice, what would it be? What if you could give your older self any advice – what would that be?

8 If you could change one part of your appearance, what would it be? Are there any ways you could do this? Would it cost money? Would it hurt? Would it be safe?

9 If you had to eat all of your meals for the rest of your life from any one international cuisine, which would it be?

10 What scares you? Why? Can anything be done about this fear?

11 If money were no object, what physical thing would you like for your next birthday?

12 What is, physically, the hardest thing you have ever done? What was hard about it? What could you have done to make it easier? Was it worth it?

13 What country in the world do you most want to visit next? Why?

14 If you could go anywhere that you have already been for a second visit, where would it be? Why?

15 Who do you need to apologise to? Why? What would you say? And who do you think owes you an apology?

16 What smells remind you of your childhood?

17 What is the most exotic thing in your fridge right now? Where does it come from? What is it used for?

18 In the hot air balloon game (in which you have to pretend that you are in a hot air balloon that is losing height and you need to discard some weight, so each person has to persuade the others that they should not be thrown overboard) why do you think you should be kept inside?

19 What would you do with an extra hour in the day?

20 When you want to be alone, where do you go?

21 Read the ingredients on the back of one of the bottles in your bathroom. Do you know what they all are?

22 Do you want your children or grandchildren to have the same kind of schooling you had?

23 What did you learn at school? Can you remember specific facts you learned and from which teacher?

24 Do you understand what your friends do in their jobs?

25 Which of your friends do you think is most likely to be a spy? What makes you think this?

26 If you needed to lie low for a bit, which friend would you trust to hide you? Do you think they would keep your secret? How long would they hide you for?

27 Is there anything you wish you were brave enough to wear? Go on, try it...

28 Has your life turned out the way you thought it would?

29 Why do you vote the way you vote? What would persuade you to vote for a different party?

30 Do all your friends have the same broad opinions? What is the most outrageous opinion held by a friend of yours? Why do you think it is outrageous?

31 What are you going to have for dinner today?

32 Go for a walk – what litter do you see? How environmentally damaging is it? Who picks it up? Who is dropping it?

33 Where are your grandparents from? Is it a long way from your home? Or do you live in the same village as them? What led you to where you are?

34 What is the most exciting thing you have ever received through the post?

35 If you won millions on the lottery, what would you do with it? Find someone who has done this.

36 Does any of your furniture need a makeover? How could you do this? On a budget? With money no object?

37 What foods don't you like? Is there a scientific reason for this? A psychological reason for this? Do other people share your dislike? If you are served it at someone else's house do you eat it anyway?

38 Who taught you to cook? How did they do it? What age were you?

39 What languages can you speak? Are they useful? Do you think differently or have a different personality in each language?

40 Your best friend has a deep dark secret – what do you think it might be?

41 Where were the clothes you are wearing today made?

42 How much could a stranger find out about you online? See how much you can find out about a stranger online – what tools do you use? What can't you find out?

43 Have you ever bullied anyone? Why? Do you feel bad about it now? Do you know what your victim is doing now?

44 Could you explain to someone over the phone how to drive your car? Try it. What steps would you break it down into?

45 Name as many types of tree as you can. Who taught you these names? Can you recognise them all?

46 Do you know how much pension you will get? Are you worried about this being enough? What can you do about this?

47 What colour is your front door? Did you choose it? Why?

48 What would improve the service in your local supermarket?

49 Who is the most successful person you know? What made them successful? Are there lessons to be learned from this? Would you want their job? Are they happy?

50 Do you know your neighbours? If not, why not? What would happen if you knocked on their door just to introduce yourself?

51 How much have you spent on clothes this year? On cosmetics? Did you mean to?

52 Who is in charge of finances in your household? Do any other members of the household know how to sort out the household accounts? If you disappeared would they be able to pay the bills, or vice versa if they are the person responsible for the accounts? What do you need to put in place to ensure this is possible?

53 What (if anything) makes you feel like a grown up?

54 What do you recommend as a hangover cure?

55 What is your most helpful labour-saving device? What would life be like without it?

56 Who would you most like to look like? How could you go about achieving this?

57 Do you have any herbs or spices in your cupboards that you have never used? Use them. What are the results? What would a chef advise you to do with them?

58 What is the biggest cause of death for your age group? How can you protect yourself from this? Find families of people who died from this.

59 Find a local business. What is the biggest challenge they are facing at the moment?

60 Can you have a week where you buy nothing other than travel and food? What do you miss? What free things do you discover?

61 What sport do you like least? Try watching some – can you see a way to find it interesting?

62 If you didn't do your current job what job would you like to do? What job do you think you'd be most likely to be doing? Are they the same? If not, why not?

63 Who has most helped you in your career? How did they do this? Do they know they helped you? Do you 'pay it forward' to others?

64 What does your pet think about all day? What does it do when you are out?

65 Do you, or anyone you know, collect anything? What is their collection worth? How did it start? Who will they leave it to in their will?

66 Can you name the capitals of all of the world's countries? Which ones can you name? Which flags can you recognise? What random facts do you know about foreign countries? Are they all true?

67 Where do the chefs you know go out for dinner? How do doctors choose their own doctor? Who cuts your hairdresser's hair?

68 Do you know any 'early adopters' (people who are always the first to get the latest technology)? What is the thing they most covet at the moment? And what are they just waiting to be invented? Similarly, who are the coolest people you know – what are they into at the moment?

69 Who do you admire and what quality is it you admire specifically (either people you know or famous people)? How can you go about achieving these qualities? Conversely, what qualities don't you like? How can you ensure you don't develop these?

70 Where do people who live on your street come from originally? What brought them here? What are your differences and what do you have in common?

71 What meats wouldn't you feel comfortable eating? Why?

72 Which world leader do you think is doing the best job? Why?

73 What small things would make your life better? Ask this of everyone you know. Could these changes be achievable?

74 Do you know any adults who really believe in things you know to be untrue (e.g. fairies). How do you know this is untrue? Why do they believe it?

75 What doesn't your partner know about you?

76 What is your favourite animal to look at in the zoo? Why? Is that animal generally happy in captivity? How is that measured?

77 What do you do differently to your parents (e.g. support a different football team, follow a different religion, cook different foods, etc.)?

78 When you are feeling low, what do you do? Do you think this could help other people too?

79 Do you have a signature dish that you frequently cook? How did it become your signature dish?

80 How many close friends do you have? Do you trust them? Do they make you feel good about yourself? How did you meet them?

81 Whose image would you like to see on a banknote and why?

82 What could be done to improve your experience when you visit your doctor?

83 How much do you give to charity? How much was your last donation and to which charity? Why did you choose them?

84 Do you have a will? If not, why not? If so, what made you make it?

85 How do you store your photos? If on a computer, do you have back-ups? How would you feel if you lost all of your photographs?

86 Are you happy? If not, what would make you happy? Is this achievable? Is it within your control or the control of others?

87 What was the first piece of music you remember buying? Do you still like it? Is it embarrassing?

88 Have you got, or have you ever owned, a pet? What was/is it? Do you like it? Does it take a lot of looking after? What do you do with it when you are on holiday?

89 What would be your ideal pet?

90 Do you know the words to your national anthem?

91 What is your New Year's resolution? What were some past resolutions you made? Did you keep them?

92 Are your shoes comfortable (literally, not metaphorically)?

93 Design your dream home. What would it look like?

94 How do you arrange the books on your shelves?

95 If you could have chosen your own name, what would it be?

96 Read the letters page of any publication you have to hand. What are people writing about and why? What do they hope to achieve by this?

97 What would you call your autobiography?

98 How much money do you think you need to live the life you want to live?

99 Impart some wisdom – what has life taught you that you can pass on to someone else?

100 Why does this list number a hundred? What is the significance of certain numbers both personally and generally? What about in other cultures?

Glossary

The words used in feature writing differ from publication to publication, writer to writer and country to country. I go into each of the following terms in detail at different stages throughout the book, but here is a quick guide to what I mean when I use the following words:

Beat

The term 'beat' is used in news to mean your specialist geographic or subject area that you become knowledgeable about and write stories about. In feature writing it can be interchangeable with 'specialism', that is, a subject area about which you often write.

Colour

'Colour' is the word used in feature writing to mean the descriptive writing that makes the reader feel as if they were there with you – the sounds and smells and details that bring to life the picture you are painting with your words.

Commission

If your editor gives you a commission this means they have agreed to publish an article written by you on a particular subject. This can be based on a pitch, in which case you will have come up with the idea, or they may come to you with an idea and ask you to write it.

Editor

In this book when I use the word 'editor' I don't mean the overall editor who is in charge of an entire publication, but a 'section editor' or 'commissioning editor' – the person in charge of a smaller part of the publication who will be able to decide whether to give you a commission or not. Therefore, when pitching, it is worth finding out the name of the relevant commissioning editor so that you can send your pitch to the right person. (A quick phone call to the publication can usually determine this, if the information isn't obvious inside the publication or on the website.) On smaller publications the overall editor may also be the commissioning editor.

Hook (also known as a 'peg')

The reason the idea is relevant for publication now.

Pitch

The outline of your idea that you give to an editor (verbally or in writing) to see whether they would like to commission you to write an article.

PR

PR stands for public relations but tends to be used by journalists to mean the person working in public relations who is representing something they want you to write about (or want you not to write about). As in, 'I got the story from a PR I'm friendly with'. PRs have many tools – events, free gifts, trips for journalists, face-to-face conversations and press releases being the ones you may be most likely to come across.

Index

academics 143
acronyms 70
adoption 118–19
Adult Fans of Lego (AFOLs) 31–2
advertisements 16, 17; *Stylist* magazine
    86–97
advertorials 92, 94, 97
Aldo 85, 97
Allen, Woody 91
Allsopp, Kirstie 80
Amazon 10
androgyny 86, 92
angle 13–15, 18, 66, 127, 159; changing
    the 60, 67, 91
animals 134
ankle socks 135
anniversaries 130, 131, 132, 134, 146
announcement columns 104
arguments 147
art 66, 68–9
audience 13–20, 66, 97–8, 127, 159;
    background information 150;
    changing the 59, 60, 68–9, 91;
    professional women in their thirties
    and forties 65–6; relating to readers
    62; tampons 22–3
Austen, Jane 23–4

background information 150
bad habits 99
Baker, Jamie 82–3
bands 37, 38
barber shops 111–12
Bath 23–4
Batt, Mike 136
BBC 7–8, 54–5, 62, 79, 133
BBC Magazine 34
beats 74, 165
beauty treatments 51, 89, 92, 93

Bell, Johanna 70
Belvedere Vodka 86
Benefits Street 67
bereavement 40–1, 43
BHS 93–4
Billy Elliot The Musical 96–7
Bland, Archie 82–4
blogs 42, 81, 144
Boaz Trust 119
books 96
Boots 93
boring subjects 103
Branson, Richard 150
bread prices 67
bromance 70
Bruges 147–8
brunch 95
builders 37, 39

Cadwalladr, Carole 10
calls to action 151
Calvin Klein 86
camper vans 108, 109
cancer 120–1
Carmichael, Laura 88
cars 87, 95
case studies 11, 13, 130, 132,
    141–2, 156
celebrities: celebrity chefs 104; clothing
    ranges 56; engagements 104; facts
    about 72; hooks 128–9, 131;
    Stylist magazine 86, 89, 97; Twitter
    comments by 80
Chabon, Michael 31
charities 118, 119–21, 123, 142, 143
chatrooms 76–7
cheese 66, 69
chefs 104
childbirth 15, 44–5

children: health problems 72; Lego 28, 30, 32, 33; life skills 112; teaching of history to 107; tooth decay 54–5; Walk to School Week 123; *see also* schools
Children with Cancer UK 120–1
Christmas 37, 39, 77, 135–6
Clark, Malcolm 122–3
climate change 45–6
clothes 100–1, 104; ankle socks 135; celebrity ranges 56; hats 74; hooks 131–2; red trousers 114; *Stylist* magazine 85–6, 89, 90, 92, 93–4; trends 48; work uniforms 87; *see also* shoes
Coca-Cola 92, 94
coffee 94, 104
colour 148–50, 165
commissioning timetables 155
commissions 153–8, 165
conclusions 151–2
confidence 2, 159
connecting ideas 26
Connery, Sean 72
Connolly, Billy 72
context 141
contraceptive pill 115
conversations, ideas from 41–2, 78, 106
cookery books 96
'co-production' 116, 117
Crabtree, James 112
cranes 111, 112
crime 55, 63, 65, 71
Cross, Michael 24–6
crying 40

Daily Express 34
Daily Mail 34, 46
Daily Mirror 75, 116
Daniels, Paul 80
Darlington, Richard 116–18
data protection 75
dating 37, 38
dental care 54–5, 93, 94, 102
dentists 55, 94, 102–3
descriptive writing 148–50, 165
The Devil Wears Prada 48
diaries, hooks 134
diarised events 128, 131
disability 41
domestic violence 133
Downton Abbey 88

East Village London 96
Eastern Daily Press 73
Easy Living 115
Ebola virus 12–13
The Economist 112
editors 9, 127, 153–5, 157–8, 165–6
electroceuticals 116
emergencies 59–60
emotions 40–1
empathy 62
ending an article 151–2
engagements 104
entertainment guides 73, 96
essays 10
European Union (EU) 58–9
Evening Standard 104
events, diarised and non-diarised 128, 131
events listings 73
experiential features 10
experts: asking 112, 142–6; readers as experts 7
'explainer' features 12, 13
eyebrows 48, 51, 111

Fabulous 108
Facebook 34, 42–3, 70
facts 147–8
family 36–7
fashion 88–9, 92, 93–4, 97, 131–2; *see also* clothes
Fear of Missing Out (FOMO) 70
features: definition of 7; ideas from 74; key components of 139–52; question being answered 7–8; types of 9–13
Federer, Roger 83
feminism 27–8, 48
Ferreiro, Laura 49
fetal medicine 44–5
film 49, 95, 96
finance 64–5
Financial Times 29, 107, 112
fingernails 99
First World War 24–6
fitness classes 107–8
flags, England 56–7
Fleming, Ian 103
Flett, Kathryn 147–8
food: bread prices 67; brunch 95; cakes 97; celebrity chefs 104; cheese 66, 69; cookery books 96; healthy eating for pregnant women 105–6; horse meat scandal 114; ice cream 77, 91,

104; jam 14–15; magazines 16; social media 42; sweets 21; Thai 97; trends 48, 104, 105
forums, online 76–7, 142, 144
Fraser, Giles 136
'Freak shows' 11
freelance writing 2, 15, 54
frenemies 70
friends 37–8, 39–42, 45–53, 78
Friends 94
frog jumping 78–9
Frost, Sadie 72
Frozen 48
Fry, Stephen 80
fuel prices 62–3
funding 24

Gallo wine 95
Gardiner, Becky 66–7
Geary, Joanna 90
Geddes, Linda 39–40, 78–9
gender 27–8, 30, 32, 33, 46; *see also* women
GlaxoSmithKline 116
Goldup, Alex 118
golf 1
Google 81
Gordon, Olivia 44–5
Greenslade, Roy 114
groups of people 21, 61–2
Guardian 10, 16, 34, 36, 53, 57, 67, 82, 105, 107, 119, 136
gyms 107–8

Häagen-Dazs 91
Habitat 91
habits, bad 99
haircuts 110–11
Hampden-White, Caroline 120–1
Hannah, Daryl 72
happiness 66, 69
Harris, Tony 121
Harry Potter 34, 80, 134
hats 74
headlines 8, 9
health care 75, 133
Heffner, Hugh 81
Henley, Jon 67
Henman, Tim 82
Heren, Louis 113
'Hey Doris' facts 114
Hilpern, Kate 36–7, 118–19
hooks 127–38, 141, 146, 153, 166

Hoover, Herbert 138
horse meat scandal 114
'How to...' features 11, 12

i100 133
ice cream 77, 91, 104
Idealia Life Serum 89
ideas 2–3, 13–14, 71–2, 84; connecting 26; from friends 37–8, 39–42, 45–53, 78; from new people, places and things 99–112; from the news 54–70; from other features 74; prompts for 159–64; recognising 83; from social media 42–4; *Stylist* magazine 85; things you'd like to do 108–9; from your own life 36–9, 44–5
immigration 58, 67
Independent 24, 34, 119, 133
Indian Ocean tsunami (2004) 140
in-house writing 15, 54
inquisitiveness 101
inspirational features 11
Institute for Public Policy Research (IPPR) 117
interior design 109
internet: finding experts 144; online chatrooms and forums 76–7; *see also* social media; websites
interviews 83, 90, 93
introductions 139–41
inventions 65, 68
investigative features 12
iPhones 106

Jaguar Land Rover 121, 122
jam 14–15
Jane Austen parade, Bath 23–4
Job Information Packs 53
jobs 53, 102, 109; *see also* work
John Frieda 93
Jolie, Angelina 105–6
Jolin, Lucy 132
Jones, Jonathan 34
journalists: help from other 84, 142, 143; public relations 117, 118, 121, 123
Jupp, Emily 23–4

Kardashians 89
Kenzo 93

Larkin, Philip 132
Latinos 58

Law Society Gazette 24–6
Lawrence, Felicity 67
leadership 51
leaflets 72, 75
leather 89
Lefort, Rebecca 80–1
Lego 27–35
Levenson, Ellie 53, 105–6
lipstick 16, 86, 87, 88, 106–7
list features 10, 13, 87
literature 96
Lively, Blake 92
Living Streets 123
local newspapers 60, 82
localisation of stories 59, 130
Lockerbie bombing 107
London 76, 91, 96
LOOK 41, 107
L'Oréal 92
Lucas, Pam 92

macaroons 104, 105
Mackenzie, Donald 64
magazines 54, 157; audiences 15–16;
　commissioning timetables 155;
　hooks 137; *Stylist* magazine 85–98
Make Votes Count 122
Mangan, Lucy 91
Marks and Spencer 89, 92, 97
massages 108, 109
maternal mortality 15
May, James 33
meetings 50, 51
Metafilter 78
military personnel 121–2
military uniforms 100
Milne, Richard 29
Minecraft 32–3
moral lessons 151
Moss, Kate 88
Mount Ararat 64
MPs' expenses scandal 122
multi case study based features 11
Mumsnet 76
music 49, 90, 133, 135–6

nails 99
NARS 86–7
National Health Service (NHS) 75
natural disasters 59–60
New Scientist 39, 78
New York Fashion Week 88
news 46, 54–70, 71, 90

news features 11
newspapers 54, 133, 157; audiences
　15–16; commissioning timetables
　155; hooks 137; local 60, 82
Nicholls, David 88
NME 49
non-diarised events 128, 131
Norfolk 73

obituaries 71
objects: getting ideas from 16, 21–6;
　Lego 27–35
Observer 147
oil prices 62–3
old age 38
Olympic Village, London 96
online chatrooms and forums 76–7
opinion 71, 151
Optrex 93
Orange Prize 134
oxytocin 40

parents, financial support for 37, 38
Parliamentary Questions 81
patches 74
Payton, Johanna 115
pegs *see* hooks
pelvic floor rehabilitation 104
Penny, Laurie 78
pens 21, 22, 87
perfume 86
personal essays 10
personal improvement features 12
perspective, getting a different 110
Peugeot 87
Phenton, Jayne 123
Phipps, Belinda 80
piercings 72
Pim, Keiron 73
Pink Stinks campaign 85–6
Pinterest 43
pitches 2, 9, 109, 153–8, 165, 166
Pitt, Brad 105–6
places, ideas from new 109, 111
plays 88
playwrights 28
police 95
politicians 56–7, 67, 81, 89, 122,
　135, 143
polls 114
poverty 134–5
pregnant women 105–6, 115
press releases 113–15, 123, 135

Prevett, Hannah 121–2
Pub Quiz Effect 148
public opinion 114
public relations (PR) 113–23, 142, 166
publications: audiences 15, 16–18,
    19, 150; dissecting 98; old 76;
    pitching 155–6; *Stylist* magazine
    85–98; timescales 133, 155; *see also*
    magazines; newspapers

questions: about objects 21–2;
    answering a question with a feature
    7–8; to ask experts 146; to ask
    friends 51–2; descriptive writing
    149–50; ideas from strangers 101;
    news events 62; six key 55–6
quotes 138, 140–1, 142–6, 152

race 29
Red 41
Reddit 78
relationships 94–5, 147
relevance 151
reportage 10, 12–13
research 25, 84, 106–7, 128, 131
reviews 71, 95, 96
Rickman, Dina 133
Rimmel 88
The Riot Club 95
Roads and Kingdoms 64
Rogers, Jude 135–6
Roma 58–9
Rubik's Cube 91
Russell, Bob 81

salon.com 34
scepticism 113
schools: adverts for 111, 112; case
    studies 141–2; class sizes 127–30,
    140–1, 152; gifts for teachers 77;
    parents' interaction with 37, 38;
    Walk to School Week 123
Scottish Independence debate 89
self-help features 12
setting the scene 140
Shadow Attorney General 56–7
shadowing 101
shoes 1, 72, 85, 97
sitcoms 94
sleep 108
Smith, Dave 119–20
social media 36, 79–80, 95; case studies
    142; expert comments 143; Fear of

Missing Out 70; food vans 104; ideas
    from 42–4; rules of tweeting 56; *see
    also* Facebook; Twitter
soldiers 121–2
solicitors 24–6
Solon, Olivia 75, 116
specialist areas 74, 165
ST Dupont pen 87
Starbucks 94
statistics 141, 147–8
staycations 70
Stewart, Patrick 72
story telling 9–10
straight features 12
strangers, ideas from 99–101
stress 39
Strictly Come Dancing 133
Stylist magazine 79, 85–98
subject 13–15, 18, 66, 127, 159;
    background information 150; boring
    subjects 103; changing the 59, 60,
    68–9, 91
Sun 34, 70, 79, 108
Sunday Telegraph 80
Sunday Times 122
surveys 113–14, 128, 131
sweets 21
synchronized swimming 18

tampons 22–3
Taylor, Elizabeth 81
teachers 77
technology 116
Telegraph 16, 34, 79, 122, 133
tennis 82–3
Tesco 93
thermomixes 104
Third Sector PR 118
Thompson, Mark 122
Thompson, Teddy 135–6
Tia Maria 90–1
The Times 36, 44–5, 104
timescales 133, 155
'toddler test' 103
tooth decay 54–5
toothpaste 94
Toy Story 48
toys 74, 91; *see also* Lego
Trainor, Meghan 133
travel 64, 91
trends 48, 73, 79, 103–5, 130, 132
trousers, red 114
Turkey 64

Twitter 79–80, 81, 85, 90, 95; expert
    comments 143; Fear of Missing Out
    70; rules of tweeting 56; Shadow
    Attorney General resignation 56, 57
Twyman, Joe 114

uniforms 87, 100
United States 57–8, 59

Vauxhall 87, 95
Virgin Galactic SpaceShipTwo 143–4,
    146, 150
vodka 86

Wade, Laura 88
WAGs 70
Ward, James 82
Warner, Hannah 72
warning features 12
websites 43, 78; audiences 15–16; BBC
    7–8, 54–5, 62; online chatrooms
    and forums 76–7; Parliamentary
    Questions 81; *see also* social media
Wheeler, Maggie 97
Williams, Pharrell 85, 86, 93, 97

Windsor, Barbara 72
wine 95
Wired 75, 116
Wish I Was Here 96
The Wombles 136
women: Fear of Missing Out 70;
    maternal mortality 15; older 92–3;
    Orange Prize 134; pregnant 105–6,
    115; professional women in their
    thirties and forties 65–6; *Strictly Come
    Dancing* 133; violence against 133
Wood, Jenny 41, 107–8
work: ideas from friends 49–50; Job
    Information Packs 53; leadership
    skills 51; meetings 50, 51;
    relationships with colleagues 37, 38;
    shadowing someone at 101; working
    abroad 108–9
Wrigley, Patrick 64

YouGov 114
Younge, Gary 57–9
YouTube 66, 68, 111

Zak, Paul 40